Protect Your Land

A guide in the things every landowner should know to protect their property rights and increase the value of their investment.

By: Randy L. Fitch, PLS

Protect Your Land – A guide in the things every landowner should know to protect their property rights and increase the value of their investment.

Published by Fitch Media

First Edition, December 2008

Editor: Brian Boone, West Egg Editing

Cover Design: Pixel Productions, Inc.

Production: Pixel Productions, Inc.

ISBN: 978-0-578-00384-9

ACKNOWLEDGMENTS

Thank you to the three reasons I enjoy life so much—you know who you are. Thanks for putting up with the thousand of hours a year dad spends at the keyboard without making him move into the garage.

Table of Contents

Section I: Protecting Your Property

Section II: Increasing Your Property's Value

SECTION I: PROTECTING YOUR PROPERTY

1

Land Ownership in the United States

Land:
an immovable and indestructible three-dimensional area
consisting of a portion of the earth's surface, the space
above and below the surface, and everything growing on or
permanently affixed to it.
Black's Law Dictionary, Eighth Edition

In the first quarter of 2008, the average cost of a new home in the United States was $293,100, while the average cost of a used home was $245,100. Very few of us who call ourselves land or homeowners own our land and home outright, thus, these hundreds of thousands of dollars that may amount to five or even 10 times our annual salary will be borrowed from a bank.

This significant financing may be in addition to a collection of other debts, possibly a car payment or two, and probably a credit card or two, or three. How about a second mortgage on your home? Or maybe a high mortgage from a refinancing or two?

Out of all these common debts, which concern you the most? Is it your credit cards? Your cars? Or is it your mortgage?

Well, for some reason, most of us are more worried about our Visa or MasterCard bill than our mortgage. Why is that? As shown above, the average cost

Interesting Tidbit

The average cost of a new home in the first quarter of 2008 was $293,100. The average cost of a used home was $245,100

of a new home in the U.S. in 2008 was around 290K, while the average credit card debt was less than 10K. And consider this: with a 30-year mortgage, you will likely pay over twice the original principal if you stay in your home for the full term. For most of us, dishing out over 600K is probably the largest investment we will make in our entire lives. Not to mention that fact that with the poor lending practices of the early twenty-first century, many loan packages were given for more than a property's long-term value.

But how much do we really know about what we are investing so much money and committing so much of our time? When we go out and purchase a car, boat, or RV, most of us understand the benefits of owning that fancy bucket of bolts. We may spend months or even years searching out just the right deal, with all the right options, the right brand and make, the right engine, the right safety equipment, etc. But with land and home, we often search based on two things: our gut instinct, and the advice of a real estate agent.

As in many industries, however, there is a large range of

knowledge and experience within the pool of real estate agents and most of us really don't perform adequate due diligence in selecting an agent. In other words, you, the hopeful buyer, who typically doesn't have any experience with title transfers, property rights, or land planning, are led by an agent who may have very little training themselves in such things, into the largest financial transaction of your life.

However, some of the possible lien holders on your land are experts. These may be your mortgage holder, your county tax collector, contractors that have worked on the property, and possibly even your neighbor. The first three many of us are aware of, but your neighbor might have raised your eyebrows a bit. Yes, your neighbor gaining rights to your land through use is not uncommon, which we'll get into later. And miss a few payments on either your mortgage or your taxes and you will soon find the gears of the machine of land law begin slowly turning as the lien holders move to collect on their investment.

Many of us treat the purchase of land like going to the doctor. We feel the complexity of the treatment is such that we just have to do what the stakeholders say. We sometimes feel that such a large transaction only happens somewhere behind heavy thick doors where silver-haired men in thousand-dollar suits pull together heavy contracts with signature lines binding us to hundreds of little clauses.

But title transfers and property rights didn't come to this world from MDs or PhDs. They originated from common landowners like you and me trying to defend their property rights in court. These court decisions, based on English Common Law, shaped the rules we live with today.

Owning land entails rights of usage, which is key to its value now and in the future. But since the purchase price is so large, most people just place their trust with the team that handles the title transfer, i.e. their real estate, a title officer, and a mortgage company's underwriter.

But most of us aren't too worried about purchasing land and home. Many of us think of our home and land as our safest investment. Land always appreciates in the long run, they say. (You can almost see the Beav's dad placating a worried Wally with that useful tidbit.) Land does tend to appreciate over a steady, long-term rate, but only if the title is sound, the property rights you think you own really exist, and you have chosen your location carefully, not only choosing the property in its current condition, but also in the condition the land will be in when you decide to sell, or even deed it to your kids. In other words, one must predict the future of the area where the property is located.

There is a bit more to determining the three most important rules in buying real estate (Location-Location-Location). You may be surprised to know that technology and an understanding of the government planning processes will allow you to predetermine the two, five, or even 10-year future of an area where you are thinking of buying.

As for title, if you thought you were safe just signing on the dotted line after going through the typical process, you are wrong.

In the last ten years, many Americans chose their land investments poorly. Many are upside-down in their homes now and struggling with rising interest rates because of signing on to an ill-advised adjustable rate mortgage (ARM). Some of us have had our blinders on from time to time when it came to purchasing our property. We were optimistic about its future and had a warm, fuzzy feeling in our tummies knowing real estate was always a safe investment. And, once we were owners, we are persistently optimistic about our land's value, and ignorant to what we could really do with it.

Signing for a parcel of land is really signing on to a whole bundle of possible tangibles. Really, a parcel of real estate is a living, multi-faceted dynamic with all sorts of possible rights and uses. In the courts, a piece of real estate is typically described as a bundle of sticks. Each stick is a right you have to use the

Information Tip

A parcel of land is a really a bundle of rights the land owner holds temporarily. At any time since the land was patented by the government to a private owner any of these rights could have been sold or lost. In the courts, this concept is described as a holding a bundle of sticks—sticks that can be bought, sold, given, taken, won or lost over the last centuries.

land, such as a right to possess the land, a right to use water, a right to use the air, a right to take minerals or other natural resources from the earth, a right to take timber from the land or farm the land, or a right to ingress or egress, which is a right dealing with access to and from your land, as well as many other rights that allow semi-complete use of a three dimensional area that radiates from the center of the Earth through your property lines and projects out into the heavens. But one must realize that any of these rights, from the time of the original land patent granting a parcel to the first owner, could have been passed away to another party.

Many of us purchase property without realizing there is a two-page list in their title report detailing easements, reservations, and restrictions upon the property. These are called encumbrances, which are a claim or liability attached to the property, such as a lien, mortgage, or a non-ownership interest, that may potentially lessen its value.

Maybe an easement called out in the title report is just for the gas line running behind the curb in front of your house. Or maybe it's for an irrigation line running through your backyard, which will prevent you from adding onto the family room like you've been promising your kids for years.

If confronted by any of the hundreds of problems that can arise as a landowner, most of us don't know what to do. When your neighbor Joe claims the 100-year-old maple tree next to your fence is a nuisance for dumping leaves in his yard and so he decides to cut all the limbs down one side of the tree, most of us, after voicing our opinion to Joe, would immediately call a lawyer. Subsequently, your land is surveyed and you discover that possibly you do own the trunk of the tree. But what does that mean? The tree is still alive, but now looks a bit like your great Aunt Marge did when she woke up after falling asleep on the makeup counter next to a leaky tube of Nair. You're $1,000 into attorneys' fees, $3,000 into land surveyor fees, and you haven't even been to court yet.

Was there something you could have done to stop this before it got ugly? Probably. But remember, it could have been much worse — a limb from that maple could have fallen on your neighbor.

Many of us dream of improving our land or our home, or even developing our land into a different state of use, such as subdividing or changing a property's zoning to make a residential property a commercial or industrial property. Maybe you've purchased a home as a rental with the idea of a zone change to drive up the value. But did you really understand the process before signing your name to hundreds of thousand of dollars of debt? Improvements can be difficult and development can be down right nasty.

For someone who doesn't understand the process, that is.

There are lengthy processes involved in any change to real estate controlled by common law, statute, or state law, as well as county or city zoning codes, each of which must be followed to make any modification to your home or land.

Did you think you live in a free country? Not even close. However, most of us enjoy the laws we've enacted; it is a good thing that a dog food plant can't be built next to your townhouse. But rules are rules and to enjoy the benefits we need to understand them and why they were enacted in the first place.

To improve or develop your land, you will need the help of the experts, and to use their skills appropriately, you should know how the system works. Whether buying, selling, improving, or developing your land, understanding the system can and will save you thousands of dollars in the long run by allowing you to effectively choose the right team, and most importantly, assign professionals with the right tasks to bring together your plans.

From improving your property to developing real estate, from property lines disputes, to easements or agreements between neighbors, it pays hugely to know the systems in place that controlled your parcel's past, control its present condition, and will control its future.

To begin, let's take a peek at how we got here.

General George—Founding Father, Landowner & Surveyor

The United States is a young country. Just over 230 years ago, the Declaration of Independence was written by Thomas Jefferson, signed by the Continental Congress, and sent by horse to General Washington, who at the moment was quite busy trying to root the British out of Boston.

With this act, our people defied the rule of an unfairly taxing monarchy and created a land where people like you and me could hold title in fee simple to the lands of America.

Most don't realize how privileged we are. Many don't realize that during the Revolutionary War, Congress offered, almost pressed upon, Washington the power of a dictator, to use whatever resources and powers the colonies had to offer in his sole and complete authority to defend the lands of the fledgling states.

Interesting Tidbit

General George Washington was given complete power by the Continental Congress to defeat the British, power he could have kept. But rather, he returned this power once the freedom of the states was won. If he had chosen differently all the land in this country would have likely remained in the hands of a monarch.

And as a matter of fact, Washington had already taken that authority, to an extent, promising soldiers stipends if they would stay on for another campaign. While Washington was famous for getting the approval of Congress before acting, in this instance circumstances demanded he take complete control.

But in the end, rather than easily take this power over the growing country, our first great leader stepped down, giving the power and land rights back to the people he had fought for.

By understanding how truly fortunate you are to be a

landowner, you can begin to realize the importance of being knowledgeable in your land's title and your subsequent rights.

While for our first general, the duty to secure our rights demanded he subject thousands of souls to the probability of terrible hardship by any number of means, like deathly cold, starvation, disease, and the iron ball or blunt stock of a musket, today, in a more peaceful respect, one can learn to own and defend their own piece of America through the best weapon available in our age: knowledge.

Wherever you live in the United States, there is a history behind your land. It was likely owned by numerous individuals before you. Each passing of the land from owner to owner required a title transfer, which likely included a deed and land description, describing the boundary of the land and any easements or encumbrances, as well as describing the intent of the seller. Was the land description the same in every transfer? Was each encumbrance listed in every transfer, or were some lost over time?

Maybe you live in a subdivision in San Louis Obispo, California, and don't know the city's street right-of-way lies only a few steps from your door, although your front yard runs a good 30 feet deep. Or possibly your ancestors owned land in Connecticut, in towns burned and pillaged by the Brits, and maybe, just maybe, you have an inheritance in the Fire Lands: 500,000 acres of Ohio set aside to compense Connecticut veterans of the Revolutionary War. Or possibly your land lies in the propionate amount of 15 states that were a part of the Louisiana Purchase of 1803, your land description recorded in French, describing land affording a superior land right to that of the later sectionalized lands surveyed under the public land survey system of the U.S.

If you're considering buying a home or parcel, great, this book will make you more savvy than most. However, even if you are already an owner, there are many things that can be done to ward off trouble before it finds you.

To begin, let's take a quick look at what controls the rights you have in a parcel of land so you can see if the condition of the parcel you are interested in may or may not be at risk. To do this, we will need to delve into that mysterious realm of legality that makes you a stakeholder in the ownership of a piece of Planet Earth. Grab your highlighter, and let's take a peek into what land title in the Unites States really amounts to.

CHAPTER 1 – KEY POINTS

✓ A parcel of land is really a bundle of rights the land owner holds temporarily. At any time since the land was patented by the government to a private owner any of these rights could have been sold or lost. In the courts, this concept is described as a holding a bundle of sticks— sticks that can be bought, sold, given, taken, won or lost over the last centuries.

✓ Lien holders such as the bank who holds your mortgage and the tax collector are experts in property rights. The only way to make full use and even grow the uses you have in your property is through gaining an understanding of these rights.

✓ An encumbrance is a claim or liability that is attached to property or some other right and that may lessen its value, such as a lien or mortgage; any property right that is not an ownership interest.

✓ Land does tend to appreciate over a steady long term rate, but only if the title is sound, the property rights you think you own really exist, and you have chosen your location carefully, not only choosing the property in its current condition, but also in the condition the land will be in when you decide to sell.

2

What Do You Really Own?
A Look at Land Title in the U.S.

A landowner really owns no more or no less than what the party who sold it to them was able to convey, and the owner before was able to convey to him, and so on and so forth.

What does this mean? Well, it means that a seller can only convey to you what was sold to them, and they only own what the previous owner before them was able to convey, which may be considerably different than what they, or their real estate agent thinks.

Confusing? Redundant? Self-evident? Not really, if you know how to do your due diligence. Let's take a look at what a land title is . . .

Title
Legal evidence of a person's ownership rights in property; an
instrument (such as a deed) that constitutes such evidence.
Black's Law Dictionary, Eighth Edition

Your title is the legal document that proves and describes what you own. Most people are comfortable with the legal document of title, for it is used as proof of other types of ownership as well, such as cars, RVs and boats. To understand land title a little better, let's take a quick look at how our country developed the system in use today to convey land from one to another:

A Quick History of Land Title in the US

Land grants in North America began immediately upon Columbus's return to Barcelona in 1492. Ferdinand and Isabella of Spain requested of Pope Alexander VI that he grant Spain the lands of the western ocean, discovered or yet to be discovered. And he did, as well as threaten excommunication to any who disputed his bull.

Realizing trouble brewing in Portugal, the Pope issued a second bull issuing to Spain only the lands westerly of a meridian (north-south line) 100 leagues (300 miles) west of the Azores and Cape Verde Islands, which are located nearly midway across the Atlantic Ocean. However, this was not agreeable to King John of Portugal.

Finally, in 1494, the Treaty of Tordesillas was signed between the two countries agreeing that Spain would get lands west of a meridian drawn between the north and south poles 370 leagues (1,110 miles) west of the Cape Verde Islands, and Portugal would hold lands east of this line. Unknown to those who developed the treaty, this line actually projects through the eastern coastline of Brazil, granting to King John a piece of South America.

Over the centuries, the primary stakeholders in the lands of North America, (Spain, Britain, and France), had settled on vast tracts of land. By the late seventeenth century, Spain in particular had claimed what would now be considered the south and southwest of the U.S.

These original land grants were not highly respected by the other immigrating countries, especially France. Twenty three years after the original papal bulls to Spain and Portugal, Francis I of France sent word to Charles V of Spain, asking:

"By what right he and the King of Portugal undertook to monopolize all the land on Earth? Had our first father, Adam, made them his sole heirs? If so, it would be more than proper for them to produce a copy of the will."

Britain Moves In

Britain's immigration into the New World began with the expedition of Sir Walter Raleigh in 1585. Then, during the early 1600s, migration from England to the U.S. began in earnest, and it is from this migration that the title law of England, known as English Common Law, was brought to North America, which is still the underlying foundation that we use today.

Early on, England granted charters to large land companies, who managed large tracts and had the authority to give grants to individuals loyal to the crown. You may remember some of these names from back in school, land companies such as the Virginia Company, the London Company, the Plymouth Company, and so on.

In early English Common Law, it was standard for land title transfers to be handled through the process of feoffment. Conveyances of freehold land would be made by feoffment and made public knowledge through a ceremony entitled the livery of seisin. In this ceremony, the feoffer would make some symbolic act to transfer the land to the feoffee, such as handing him a twig or chunk of sod followed by a verbal statement transferring ownership to another. However, the colonists did not typically continue this tradition in the new states.

The colonists quickly realized they needed a better system of keeping track of land title. In Connecticut in 1639 it became required by law to record with the public all conveyances of land. A system of public disclosure of land transfers was adopted and picked up by the other colonies as time went on.

Information Tip

Deeds, which are the evidence of title transfer, are available at your local county courthouse. With some diligent research, one can trace their parcels chain of title to its inception through government patent.

This system lives on today. In the U.S., land title must be transferred in writing through a deed and recorded in the local county courthouse. These deed records are available to the public. The process of recording these title transfers is commonly known as giving constructive notice of the title transfer.

Information Tip

To transfer title of a parcel of land, a deed is recorded with the county courthouse. This is called giving constructive notice of the transfer.

During the colonial era, many settlers gained title through a process of squatting. In 1684, land squatters petitioned King Charles that their holdings be recognized as legal. He agreed, so long as the tenants pay land rent of one shilling per acre. The sheriff who successfully collected received ten percent of the taking. Between the years of 1632 and 1689, land grants for individuals ranged from 350 acres to as large as 20,000 acres. Thus, it appears England was fairly happy to grant ownership of American soil, so long as they could profit from it.

The father of our country was deeply involved in land grabbing. In correspondence to his friend William Crawford, George Washington wrote, "Any person who neglects the present opportunity of hunting out good lands and in some measure marking and distinguishing them for their own, will never regain it." Washington goes on to let his friend know that if he finds suitable lands that Washington will secure them as soon as possible. He advises his friend to locate land "snugly under pretense of hunting game."

Crawford later writes back to Washington, saying, "There will be no possibility of taking up such quantity of land as you want near Fort Pitt, as there is such numbers of people looking for land, and one taking each other's land from him. As soon as a man's back is turned another is on his land. The man that is strong and able to make others afraid of him seems to have the best chance as times go now."

Our future president later traveled to Pennsylvania. Utilizing a court action, he evicted squatters on land he had acquired from Native Americans. To Jacob Read of the Continental Congress, he wrote: "Such is the rage for speculating in, and forestalling of, lands northwest of the Ohio, that scarce a valuable spot within a tolerable distance of it is left without a claimant. Men now talk with as much facility of five hundred thousand acres as a gentleman would formerly do of a thousand."

Today, land title in the US is conveyed from one person to the next through an instrument called a deed. As mentioned prior, these deeds are required to be recorded with your local county authority.

There are many different types of deeds, some of the most common being the Warranty Deed, the Grant Deed, the Bargain and Sale Deed, and the Quitclaim Deed, each of which we'll cover.

Deeds, as a whole, contain certain elements, such as the name of the current owner (the Grantor), the name or names of the receiving party (the Grantee), a description of the land, which allows a land surveyor to find the parcel's position on the ground, and also any things that might give or take away rights to the land.

Protection Tip

Always have your title officer look into each encumbrance listed in the preliminary title report. Verify the meaning and location of any encumbrance prior to purchase.

A deed may contain a term like "excepting therefrom," followed by a description of an easement for your neighbor for a road to his house, or a description of a pipeline easement across your land for the neighbor to draw water from a community well, which takes away from your title.

This can get a bit sticky, because often times the positives or negatives to the title may just refer you on to other documents recorded in the county courthouse. A deed may just show an easement in benefit of a power company recorded in a certain page and book in the county records. An example might read, "excluding therefrom: an easement for the transmission of power, recorded in document such and such in such and such county in 1943." Upon locating this document in the county archives one may find a description of a 20 foot-wide easement, lying on each side of the constructed power line.

What does this mean and how do you know where the easement is on your property? You may not see an overhead power line on your property. Has the line been moved over the last six or so decades? Is there an underground power line you don't see? In this instance, a power company may have never even constructed the line. Sometimes, power companies would buy blanket easements over large areas when developing their systems. The line may not even cross your land, but maybe at one time it did and the power company, knowing this, is considering a new project using their old easement that would devastate the plans you have for a new house.

The key is to determine if the easement really encumbers your property and where it is located prior to purchasing. Many times, the utility company will locate lines across your property if you request. If there is no utility crossing your land, but an easement exists that crosses your property, there may be a possibility of reversion of title, which could disallow the easement for lack of intended use.

It is a land surveyor's job to determine the position of easements described in deeds. They have the education and experience, and are certified to interpret and retrace deed records as well as locate these easements in the field.

While no landowner should attempt to locate easements from deeds, every landowner should know how deeds are created, recorded, and how to locate these records. It is a powerful tool to be able to check through the events that have transpired in a parcel's history.

Many times, one has to track down an entire chain of historical documents to determine everything that has transpired to affect the available rights on a piece of land. Many times in the purchase of land, one can put this research off on the seller, requesting he prove a clear title prior to purchase. This goes beyond the standard title insurance loan policy, which I will cover in the next chapter.

There are land surveyors, title officers, and land attorneys that, for a reasonable fee, will thoroughly research the title and deed to a parcel. Within these professions, this is known as researching the chain of title, or in other words, going back through the chain of records to investigate every known act that has changed the rights held by the current owner.

> **Protection Tip**
>
> Land title officers, attorneys, and surveyors can research a parcel's *chain of title* prior to purchase. This will allow them to identify any possible encumbrances missed in the preliminary title report.

Again, an owner can only pass on to you what they own. Sometimes, wrapping our mind around this fact is difficult. It's hard to fathom that just because you purchased a piece of land, it does not mean you have the same rights to your land as your neighbor has to his. For most, this concept can even be a little scary. However, title insurance and warranty deeds offer some protection. First, let's look into the mechanism that many believe protect their property and subsequent rights to it.

CHAPTER 2 – KEY POINTS

✓ A land title is legal evidence of a person's ownership right in property; an instrument (such as a deed) that constitutes such evidence.

✓ Deeds, when recorded with the county recorder's office, give what is known as constructive notice of title transfers. They are also used to give notice of rights transfers such as granting easements and rights of way.

✓ When purchasing land a title company will issue a title report on the parcel listing all the encumbrances. It is critical to have these encumbrances researched and identified prior to closing the deal.

✓ It's the job of the licensed land surveyor to determine the position of easements on the ground. They have the education, experience, and are certified to interpret and retrace deed records.

✓ Land title officers, attorneys, and surveyors can research a parcel's chain of title prior to purchase. This will allow them to identify any possible encumbrances missed in the preliminary title report.

3

Title Insurance

An agreement to indemnify against loss arising from a defect in title to real property, usually issued to the buyer of the property by the title company.
Black's Law Dictionary, Eighth Edition

Most of us soon-to-be or existing landowners have heard of title insurance. Title insurance is insurance to protect you against buying something other than what the title or deed appears to convey. Maybe there are undisclosed back taxes or possibly a lien against the property. Title insurance can protect a buyer against these possible encumbrances. Title insurance can protect against a grantor/seller from attempting to convey the property unethically, such as in instances where the seller is trying to sell something he doesn't hold clear title to, but it doesn't typically protect a buyer against other problems such as possible cases of adverse possession or unwritten easements, which we'll get into a bit later.

Title insurance comes in three basic forms: the loan policy, the owner's policy, and the homeowner's policy. Here are the basic elements of each:

1.   **The Loan Policy** – It protects only one party, which is the lender. The bank will require this prior to funding your loan. This insurance protects the lender in case the title to the property comes into question after the transaction. The policy amount is only for the amount of the loan and decreases as the loan balance decreases over time. This may be the only policy issued in a real estate transaction.

2.   **The Owner's Policy** – This is a separate policy purchased for an additional fee at closing. It is up to the buyer to request an owner's policy. This form of title insurance warrants that the title is clear to sell, in other words the seller does indeed hold the ownership he or she says. It also warrants that there are no liens against the property. For example, an unpaid contractor who worked on the property can place a lien on the property if not paid in full for their work. This debt must be cleared prior to closing. This type of policy will also verify there are no outstanding taxes owed on the property, that there are no errors or omissions in the deed, and that there are no unknown heirs to the property. This insurance policy will automatically pass on to any heirs.

3.   **The Homeowner's Policy** – This is a policy that will provide additional coverage beyond the standard owner's policy. One should

check with their title company to see what extended coverage they offer and then choose accordingly.

A buyer should note that he or she doesn't have to pay for the policy themselves. Providing a homeowner's policy can be made a contingency for the seller to provide.

As I mentioned previously, many of us believe as buyers or owners that the process used to purchase land through title gives them complete protection. However, the common loan policy only covers the bank. And, there are problems title insurance won't protect against. (I will go into these particular items in more detail in future chapters.)

But first, let's take a quick look at how experienced buyers limit their liability; let's look at how the big boys on the block buy land.

Limiting Liability when Purchasing Land

Large companies who invest in land know all about liability. They understand that typical title insurance, or a loan policy, isn't there to protect them, but rather the mortgage company agreeing to lend large sums of money while holding land as collateral. They also realize that the same mortgage company, especially after the mistakes they made over the last few years, will only lend typically 80% of the real worth of a parcel of land, ensuring that if they have to take the land and resell it, their investment will be somewhat safe. Knowing this, real estate investors take a couple of additional steps when buying land.

The Limited Liability Corporation or LLC

This is the type of corporation most land investors use to purchase land. As the name implies, the LLC limits the liability of the shareholders of the LLC. If something goes bad, the corporation is liable for damages, while the rest of the owner's assets are protected. What could cause a drastic difference in what the investor thinks the property is worth? Simply an undiscovered problem, like fuel tanks from a farmer's fueling station lying five feet under the ground.

Typically, it isn't wise to use an LLC when purchasing a home you plan to live in because it will void the owner-occupy tax benefits. Under today's laws, if a homeowner lives in his home for two years and then sells it, they do not have to pay taxes on any profits. However, by holding the parcel in the name of a LLC, the property will likely be considered an investment to the IRS, voiding such benefits.

But there are times when a LLC should be used, even for an individual like you or me, and that is when purchasing a rental or investment property. The idea is to hold the property in someone else's name other than your own, in this instance a corporation's, for additional protection from unknowns on the property, and for other obvious reasons if you're planning on allowing others to live on the land, which comes with its own inherit liabilities.

ALTA ACSM Land Title Surveys

The American Land Title Association ALTA was founded in 1907 and is a national trade association that represents the title insurance industry. The American Congress on Surveying and Mapping or ACSM is a similar organization that represents the land surveying profession. The ALTA and ACSM work to develop policies and guidelines that allow for a comprehensive review of a parcel's history. One of these guidelines developed by the ALTA and the National Society of Professional Surveyors or NSPS, a division of the ACSM, is the ALTA ACSM Land Title Survey. What follows are the current guidelines for this type of survey.

2005 MINIMUM STANDARD DETAIL REQUIREMENTS FOR ALTA/ACSM LAND TITLE SURVEYS
as adopted by
American Land Title Association
and
National Society of Professional Surveyors
(a member organization of the American Congress on Surveying and Mapping)

It is recognized that members of the American Land Title Association (ALTA) have specific needs, peculiar to title insurance matters, which require particular information for acceptance by title insurance companies when said companies are asked to insure title to land without exception as to the many matters which might be discoverable from survey and inspection and not be evidenced by the public records. In the general interest of the public, the surveying profession, title insurers and abstracters, ALTA and the National Society of Professional Surveyors, Inc. (NSPS) jointly promulgate and set forth such details and criteria for standards. It is recognized and understood that local and state standards or standards of care, which surveyors in those respective jurisdictions are bound by, may augment, or even require variations to the standards outlined herein. Where conflicts between the standards outlined herein and any jurisdictional statutes or regulations occur, the more restrictive requirement shall apply. It is also recognized that title insurance companies are entitled to rely on the survey furnished to them to be of an appropriate professional quality, both as to completeness and as to accuracy. It is equally recognized that for the performance of a survey, the surveyor will be provided with appropriate data which can be relied upon in the preparation of the survey.

For a survey of real property and the plat or map of the survey to be acceptable to a title insurance company for purposes of insuring title to said real property free and clear of survey matters (except those matters disclosed by the survey and indicated on the plat or map), certain specific and pertinent information shall be presented for the distinct and clear understanding between the client (insured), the title insurance company (insurer), and the surveyor (the person professionally responsible for the survey). These requirements are:

1.	The client shall request the survey or arrange for the survey to be requested and shall provide a written authorization to proceed with the survey from the person responsible for paying for the survey. Unless specifically authorized in writing by the insurer, the insurer shall not be responsible for any costs associated with the preparation of the survey. The request shall specify that an "**ALTA/ACSM LAND TITLE SURVEY**" is required and shall designate which of the optional items listed in Table A are to be incorporated. The request shall set forth the record description of the property to be surveyed or, in the case of an original survey, the record description of the parent parcel that contains the property to be surveyed. Complete copies of the record description of the property (or, in the case of an original survey, the parent parcel), any record easements benefiting the property; the record easements or servitudes and covenants burdening the property ("Record Documents"); documents of record referred to in the Record Documents; and any other documents containing desired appropriate information affecting the property being surveyed and to which the survey shall make reference shall be provided to the surveyor for notation on the plat or map of survey.

2.	The plat or map of such survey shall bear the name, address, telephone number, and signature of the professional land surveyor who performed the survey, his or her official seal and registration number, the date the survey was completed, the dates of all of the surveyor's revisions and the caption "ALTA/ACSM Land Title Survey" with the certification set forth in paragraph 8.

3.	An "**ALTA/ACSM LAND TITLE SURVEY**" shall be in accordance with the then-current "Accuracy Standards for Land Title Surveys" ("Accuracy Standards") as adopted, from time to time by the National Society of Professional Surveyors and the American Land Title Association and incorporated herein by reference.

4.	On the plat or map of an "**ALTA/ACSM LAND TITLE SURVEY**," the survey boundary shall be drawn to a convenient scale, with that scale clearly indicated. A graphic scale, shown in feet or meters or both, shall be included. A north arrow shall be shown and when practicable, the plat or map of survey shall be oriented so that north is at the top of the drawing. Symbols or abbreviations used shall be identified on the face of the plat or map by use of a legend or other means. If necessary for clarity, supplementary or exaggerated diagrams shall be presented accurately on the plat or map. The plat or map shall be a minimum size of 8½ by 11 inches.

5.	The survey shall be performed on the ground and the plat or map of an "**ALTA/ACSM LAND TITLE SURVEY**" shall contain, in addition to the required items already specified above, the following applicable information:

(a)	All data necessary to indicate the mathematical dimensions and relationships of the boundary represented, with angles given directly or by bearings, and with the length and radius of each curve, together with elements necessary to mathematically define each curve. The point of beginning of the surveyor's description shall be shown as well as the remote point of beginning if different. A bearing base shall refer to some well-fixed line, so that the bearings may be easily re-established. The North arrow shall be referenced to its bearing base and should that bearing base differ from record title, that difference shall be noted.

(b)	When record bearings or angles or distances differ from measured bearings, angles or distances, both the record and measured bearings, angles, and distances shall be clearly indicated. If the record description fails to form a mathematically closed figure, the surveyor shall so indicate.

(c)	Measured and record distances from corners of parcels surveyed to the nearest right-of-way lines of streets in urban or suburban areas, together with recovered lot corners and evidence of lot corners, shall be noted. For streets and highways abutting the property surveyed, the name, the width and location of pavement relative to the nearest boundary line of the surveyed tract, and the width of existing rights of way, where available from the controlling jurisdiction, shall be shown. Observable evidence of access (or lack thereof) to such abutting streets or highways shall be indicated. Observable evidence of private roads shall be so indicated. Streets abutting the premises, which have been described in Record Documents, but not physically opened, shall be shown and so noted.

(d)   The identifying titles of all recorded plats, filed maps, right-of-way maps, or similar documents which the survey represents, wholly or in part, shall be shown with their appropriate recording data, filing dates and map numbers, and the lot, block, and section numbers or letters of the surveyed premises. For non-platted adjoining land, names, and recording data identifying adjoining owners as they appear of record shall be shown. For platted adjoining land, the recording data of the subdivision plat shall be shown. The survey shall indicate platted setback or building restriction lines which have been recorded in subdivision plats or which appear in Record Documents which have been delivered to the surveyor. Contiguity, gores, and overlaps along the exterior boundaries of the surveyed premises, where ascertainable from field evidence or Record Documents, or interior to those exterior boundaries, shall be clearly indicated or noted. Where only a part of a recorded lot or parcel is included in the survey, the balance of the lot or parcel shall be indicated.

(e)   All evidence of monuments shall be shown and noted to indicate which were found and which were placed. All evidence of monuments found beyond the surveyed premises on which establishment of the corners of the surveyed premises are dependent, and their application related to the survey shall be indicated.

(f)   The character of any and all evidence of possession shall be stated and the location of such evidence carefully given in relation to both the measured boundary lines and those established by the record. An absence of notation on the survey shall be presumptive of no observable evidence of possession.

(g)   The location of all buildings upon the plot or parcel shall be shown and their locations defined by measurements perpendicular to the nearest perimeter boundaries. The precision of these measurements shall be commensurate with the Relative Positional Accuracy of the survey as specified in the current Accuracy Standards for ALTA/ACSM Land Title Surveys. If there are no buildings erected on the property being surveyed, the plat or map shall bear the statement, "No buildings." Proper street numbers shall be shown where available.

(h)   All easements evidenced by Record Documents which have been delivered to the surveyor shall be shown, both those burdening and those benefiting the property surveyed, indicating recording information. If such an easement cannot be located, a note to this effect shall be included. Observable evidence of easements and/or servitudes of all kinds, such as those created by roads; rights-of-way; water courses; drains; telephone, telegraph, or electric lines; water, sewer, oil or gas pipelines on or across the surveyed property and on adjoining properties if they appear to affect the surveyed property, shall be located and noted. If the surveyor has knowledge of any such easements and/or servitudes, not observable at the time the present survey is made, such lack of observable evidence shall be noted. Surface indications, if any, of underground easements and/or servitudes shall also be shown.

(i)   The character and location of all walls, buildings, fences, and other visible improvements within five feet of each side of the boundary lines shall be noted. Without expressing a legal opinion, physical evidence of all encroaching structural appurtenances and projections, such as fire escapes, bay windows, windows and doors that open out, flue pipes, stoops, eaves, cornices, areaways, steps, trim, etc., by or on adjoining property or on abutting streets, on any easement or over setback lines shown by Record Documents shall be indicated with the extent of such encroachment or projection. If the client wishes to have additional information with regard to appurtenances such as whether or not such appurtenances are independent, division, or party walls and are plumb, the client will assume the responsibility of obtaining such permissions as are necessary for the surveyor to enter upon the properties to make such determinations.

(j)   Driveways, alleys and other ways of access on or crossing the property must be shown. Where there is evidence of use by other than the occupants of the property, the surveyor must so indicate on the plat or map. Where driveways or alleys on adjoining properties encroach, in whole or in part, on the property being surveyed, the surveyor must so indicate on the plat or map with appropriate measurements.

(k)   As accurately as the evidence permits, the location of cemeteries and burial grounds (i) disclosed in the Record Documents provided by client or (ii) observed in the process of performing the field work for the survey, shall be shown.

(l)   Ponds, lakes, springs, or rivers bordering on or running through the premises being surveyed shall be shown.

6.   As a minimum requirement, the surveyor shall furnish two sets of prints of the plat or map of survey to the title insurance company or the client. If the plat or map of survey consists of more than one sheet, the sheets shall be numbered, the total number of sheets indicated and match lines be shown on each sheet. The prints shall be on durable and dimensionally stable material of a quality standard acceptable to the title insurance company. The record title description of the surveyed tract, or the description provided by the client, and any new description prepared by the surveyor must appear on the face of the plat or map or otherwise accompany the survey. When, in the opinion of the surveyor, the results of the survey differ significantly from the record, or if a fundamental decision related to the boundary resolution is not clearly reflected on the plat or map, the surveyor may explain this information with notes on the face of the plat or map or in accompanying attachments. If the relative positional accuracy of the survey exceeds that allowable, the surveyor shall explain the site conditions that resulted in that outcome with a note on the face of the map or plat.

7.   Water boundaries necessarily are subject to change due to erosion or accretion by tidal action or the flow of rivers and streams. A realignment of water bodies may also occur due to many reasons such as deliberate cutting and filling of bordering lands or by avulsion. Recorded surveys of natural water boundaries are not relied upon by title insurers for location of title.

When a property to be surveyed for title insurance purposes contains a natural water boundary, the surveyor shall measure the location of the boundary according to appropriate surveying methods and note on the plat or map the date of the measurement and the caveat that the boundary is subject to change due to natural causes and that it may or may not represent the actual location of the limit of title. When the surveyor is aware of changes in such boundaries, the extent of those changes shall be identified.

8. When the surveyor has met all of the minimum standard detail requirements for an ALTA/ACSM Land Title Survey, the following certification shall be made on the plat:

To (name of client), (name of lender, if known), (name of title insurance company, if known), (name of others as instructed by client):

This is to certify that this map or plat and the survey on which it is based were made in accordance with the "Minimum Standard Detail Requirements for ALTA/ACSM Land Title Surveys," jointly established and adopted by ALTA and NSPS in 2005, and includes Items   of Table A thereof. Pursuant to the Accuracy Standards as adopted by ALTA and NSPS and in effect on the date of this certification, undersigned further certifies that in my professional opinion, as a land surveyor registered in the State of _____, the Relative Positional Accuracy of this survey does not exceed that which is specified therein.

Date: (signed)   (seal)
                          Registration No.

NOTE: If, as otherwise allowed in the Accuracy Standards, the Relative Positional Accuracy exceeds that which is specified therein, the following certification shall be made on the plat:

To (name of client), (name of lender, if known), (name of title insurance company, if known), (name of others as instructed by client):

This is to certify that this map or plat and the survey on which it is based were made in accordance with the "Minimum Standard Detail Requirements for ALTA/ACSM Land Title Surveys," jointly established and adopted by ALTA and NSPS in 2005, and includes Items   of Table A thereof. Pursuant to the Accuracy Standards as adopted by ALTA and NSPS and in effect on the date of this certification, undersigned further certifies that in my professional opinion, as a land surveyor registered in the State of _____, the maximum Relative Positional Accuracy is _____ feet.

Date: (signed)   (seal)
                          Registration No.

The 2005 Minimum Standard Detail Requirements for ALTA/ACSM Land Title Surveys are effective January 1, 2006. As of that date, all previous versions of the Minimum Standard Detail Requirements for ALTA/ACSM Land Title Surveys are superseded by these 2005 standards.

Adopted by the American Land Title Association on October 5, 2005.
Adopted by the Board of Directors, National Society of Professional Surveyors on October 24, 2005.
American Land Title Association, 1828 L St., N.W., Suite 705, Washington, D.C. 20036.
National Society of Professional Surveyors, Inc., 6 Montgomery Village Avenue, Suite 403, Gaithersburg, MD 20879

TABLE A
OPTIONAL SURVEY RESPONSIBILITIES AND SPECIFICATIONS

NOTE: The items of Table A must be negotiated between the surveyor and client. It may be necessary for the surveyor to qualify or expand upon the description of these items, e.g., in reference to Item 6, there may be a need for an interpretation of a restriction. The surveyor cannot make a certification on the basis of an interpretation or opinion of another party. Items 16, 17 and 18 are only for use on projects for the U.S. Department of Housing and Urban Development (HUD).

If checked, the following optional items are to be included in the ALTA/ACSM LAND TITLE SURVEY, except as otherwise negotiated:

1. _____ Monuments placed (or a reference monument or witness to the corner) at all major corners of the boundary of the property, unless already marked or referenced by an existing monument or witness to the corner.

2. _____ Vicinity map showing the property surveyed in reference to nearby highway(s) or major street intersection(s).

3. _____ Flood zone designation (with proper annotation based on federal Flood Insurance Rate Maps or the state or local equivalent, by scaled map location and graphic plotting only.)

4. _____ Gross land area (and other areas if specified by the client).

5. _____ Contours and the datum of the elevations.

6. _____ List setback, height, and floor space area restrictions disclosed by applicable zoning or building codes (beyond those required under paragraph 5d of these standards). If none, so state. The source of such information must be disclosed. See "Note" above.

7. _____ (a) Exterior dimensions of all buildings at ground level

    (b) Square footage of:

        _____ (1) exterior footprint of all buildings at ground level

        _____ (2) gross floor area of all buildings; or

        _____ (3) other areas to be defined by the client

    _____ (c) Measured height of all buildings above grade at a defined location. If no defined location is provided, the point of measurement shall be shown.

8. _____ Substantial, visible improvements (in addition to buildings) such as billboards, signs, parking structures, swimming pools, etc.

9. _____ Parking areas and, if striped, the striping and the type (e.g.

handicapped, motorcycle, regular, etc.) and number of parking spaces.

10. _____ Indication of access to a public way on land such as curb cuts and driveways, and to and from waters adjoining the surveyed tract, such as boat slips, launches, piers and docks..

11. _____ Location of utilities (representative examples of which are shown below) existing on or serving the surveyed property as determined by:
_____ (a) Observed evidence

_____ (b) Observed evidence together with evidence from plans obtained from utility companies or provided by client, and markings by utility companies and other appropriate sources (with reference as to the source of information)
- railroad tracks and sidings;
- manholes, catch basins, valve vaults or other surface indications of subterranean uses;
- wires and cables (including their function, if readily identifiable) crossing the surveyed premises, all poles on or within ten feet of the surveyed premises, and the dimensions of all crossmembers or overhangs affecting the surveyed premises; and
- utility company installations on the surveyed premises.

12. _____ Governmental Agency survey-related requirements as specified by the client.

13. _____ Names of adjoining owners of platted lands.

14. _____ The distance to the nearest intersecting street as designated by the client

15. _____ Rectified orthophotography, photogrammetric mapping, laser scanning and other similar products, tools or technologies may be utilized as the basis for the location of certain features (excluding boundaries) where ground measurements are not otherwise necessary to locate those features to an appropriate and acceptable accuracy relative to a nearby boundary. The surveyor shall (a) discuss the ramifications of such methodologies (e.g. the potential accuracy and completeness of the data gathered thereby) with the title company, lender and client prior to the performance of the survey and, (b) place a note on the face of the survey explaining the source, date, relative accuracy and other relevant qualifications of any such data.

16. _____ Observable evidence of earth moving work, building construction or building additions within recent months.

17. _____ Any changes in street right-of-way lines either completed or proposed, and available from the controlling jurisdiction. Observable evidence of recent street or sidewalk construction or repairs.

18. _____ Observable evidence of site use as a solid waste dump, sump or

sanitary landfill.

One can quickly see the investigation involved in this type of survey is exhaustive and includes time on the ground to determine what liability may be incurred when purchasing a parcel of land.

An ALTA ACSM Land Title Survey costs many thousands of dollars to perform, which is why it is typically used for high-dollar commercial land purchases. Possibly, this cost can be made a contingency in an offer for purchase. With purchasing real estate along the perimeter of communities or along older roadways, it may be wise to pursue this type of survey, the reason being that there may have been commercial activities on the land, or it may include old easements from farming activities.

However, many of the problems uncovered in this type of survey can be determined by simply knowing what to look for. To do this will require familiarizing yourself with the written and unwritten records that control a property's available rights. To begin, let's take a look at the instrument used to convey land title: the *deed*.

CHAPTER 3 – KEY POINTS

✓ Title Insurance in an agreement to indemnify against loss arising from a defect in title to real property, usually issued to the buyer of the property by the title company.

✓ Title Insurance Comes in Three Basic Forms:

   o A *loan policy* protects only one party, which is the lender. The bank will require this prior to funding your loan. This insurance protects the lender in case the title to the property comes into question after the transaction. The policy amount is only for the amount of the loan and decreases as the loan balance decreases over time. This may be the only policy issued in a real estate transaction.

   o An *owner's policy* is a separate policy purchased for an additional fee at closing. It is up to the buyer to request an owner's policy. This form of title insurance warrants that the title is clear to sell, in other words the seller does indeed hold the ownership he or she says. It also warrants that there are no liens against the property. For example, an unpaid contractor who worked on the property can place a lien on the property if not paid in full for their work. This debt must be cleared prior to closing. This type of policy will also verify there are no outstanding taxes owed on the property, that there are no errors or omissions in the deed, and that there are no unknown heirs to the property. This insurance policy will automatically pass on to any heirs.

o A *homeowner's* policy is a policy that will provide additional coverage beyond the standard owner's policy. One should check with their title company to see what extended coverage they offer and then choose accordingly.

✓ Limited Liability Corporations and ALTA ACSM Land Title Surveys offer additional protection when purchasing land.

RANDY L. FITCH, PLS

4

Deeds: The Instrument of Title

Deed
A written instrument by which land is conveyed.
At common law, any written instrument that is signed, sealed,
and delivered and that conveys some interest in property.
Black's Law Dictionary, Eighth Edition

As we looked at earlier, title insurance is one mode of protection in buying land. Another form of protection is through the use of a Warranty Deed, the strongest of deeds, and one that you should verify is being used when you are buying land. Why? Just as the name suggests, this type of deed contains certain warranties. Most sellers don't realize the obligations set down by a warranty deed. Regardless, as a buyer, it should be made mandatory.

Let's take a peek at a warranty deed, other types of deeds, and how they all differ.

The Warranty Deed

The Warranty Deed consists of three individual warranties to protect the buyer:

1)   **Covenant of Seisin:** This means that the seller warrants ownership of the property and the ability to convey it.

2)   **Covenant Against Encumbrances:** The seller is warranting against any encumbrances not listed in the deed. There may be encumbrances listed in the deed, however, such as statements like "excepting therefrom an easement for a nuclear power plant." However, the seller is warranting against encumbrances not made evident by the face of the deed, such as back taxes, loans, and liens.

3)   **Covenant of Quiet Enjoyment:** In this warranty, the seller is obligated to defend the title if claims by a third party pop up against the title down the road.

Knowing this, pray tell, why isn't a Warranty Deed the staple of land transactions? In many cases it is. But if a truly ugly situation arises, such as a neighbor claiming a part of your land by adverse possession or prescriptive easement, will the other kinds of warranties hold any water? Maybe not.

Protection Tip

Always verify a Warranty Deed will be used when purchasing land. A warranty deed provides the most protection to you the buyer.

The Grant Deed

The grant deed contains three protections as well:

1) It guarantees the title holder has not previously conveyed the title to any one else.

2) It guarantees that there are no other encumbrances other than what is shown in the deed.

3) It guarantees to the seller to convey any title to the buyer received after the purchase date.

This type of deed does not, however, provide a warranty that the existing owner holds a clear title to the property being sold. Only the Warranty Deed makes that provision.

The Bargain and Sale Deed

Another type of deed is the Bargain and Sale Deed, which basically conveys property without warranties or guarantees; the owner offers nothing as to the title of the property. This type of deed is commonly used by government agencies, executors of estates, fiduciaries, and in foreclosure, sales by sheriffs for unpaid taxes and by referees for delinquent payments. You can see the theme here: The title holder has no need or desire to warrant what they are selling.

Once, when researching the chain of title of a piece of land I was considering purchasing, I noticed that a Bargain and Sale Deed had once been used. Upon further research, I realized the seller, who was also a broker, had sold part of his interest in the parcel to another broker. Broker 1 had acquired the parcel with a Warranty Deed, but then sold to Broker 2 1/2 his interest in the parcel with a Bargain and Sale Deed. I discovered I was purchasing from two brokers, but being as I could trace the fact that Broker 1 had purchased the property with a Warranty Deed, I would purchase so long as a Warranty Deed was also used in my transaction.

The Quit-Claim Deed

One final common form of deed is the Quit-Claim Deed. This type of deed is really a different animal—it conveys whatever interest a person may or may not have in a property, but gives no warranty to title and makes no claim as the seller holding title, which is key. Really, this is an instrument that can convey anything a seller may or may not own. This is the kind of deed associated with those old stories of salesmen selling the Brooklyn Bridge to a naive buyer. The danger is in not understanding that this type of deed doesn't warrant any ownership of the seller. The buyer agrees to the sale, thinking that because someone is selling them an apparent something with a legal deed that it means the seller actually has to the right to sell it.

A Quit-Claim Deed just conveys whatever interest one has to another. And, if the seller acquires interest in the property after the transaction, then this interest remains his or hers.

Protection Tip

If a new or unknown interest in land is realized after the sale, it belongs to the new owner except if a Quit Claim Deed is used. With a Quit Claim Deed, the new or unknown interest stays with the seller.

This deed is commonly used in divorces for one spouse to transfer interest to another. It also may be used when preparing for a living trust or estate to transfer interest into the trust. Another use of this deed is to allow two neighbors to settle a problematic property line by signing Quit-Claim deeds to each other for any interest on their side of an agreed upon line, such as a fence or wall.

It matters which type of deed is used to grant title and it pays to understand the types of deeds and what they do. Warranty Deeds, as we've seen, offer some protection, but what if a parcel's boundary fences are not built along the parcel lines described in your deed? Or, what if a driveway providing access to a parcel was accidentally built on someone else's land? Well, the title is not defective, so a Warranty Deed or typical title insurance won't help.

As different types of deeds convey property in different ways, so do the elements within a deed determine the boundary lines and rights to a parcel of land. To begin to come to grips with the many facets of property rights and how they can change over time, let's first look at how land is described and limited by the deed.

CHAPTER 4 – KEY POINTS

✓ A deed is a written instrument by which land is conveyed. At common law, any written instrument that is signed, sealed, and delivered and that conveys some interest in property.

✓ The more common forms of deeds are:

- o The Warranty Deed
- o The Grant Deed
- o The Bargain & Sale Deed
- o The Quit Claim Deed

✓ The Warranty Deed is the strongest of deeds and one you should verify is being used when you are buying land.

✓ The Warranty Deed contains three warranties to protect the buyer:

- o *Covenant of Seisin:* This means that the seller warrants ownership of the property and the ability to convey it.

- o *Covenant Against Encumbrances:* The seller is warranting against any encumbrances not listed in the deed. There may be encumbrances listed in the deed however, such as statements like excepting therefrom an easement for a nuclear power plant, however, the seller is warranting against encumbrances not made evident by the face of the deed, such as back taxes, loans and liens.

o *Covenant of Quiet Enjoyment:* In this warranty, the seller is obligated to defend the title if claims by a third party pop up against the title down the road.

5

Land Boundaries

In the primeval forest, particularly in the plant kingdom,
there are no boundaries between living things.
Plants do not do not create boundaries to separate themselves.
Animals—especially humans—create boundaries.
Brown's Boundary Control & Legal Principles, Fifth Edition

English Common Law was used as the basis of how land was originally afforded, delegated, sold, and given to the landowners of the early U.S. However, much of what is now the U.S. was not owned by the English, but by, of course, the native tribes, although they did not consider themselves landowners in the same sense we do, and later by France, Spain, and Mexico. And being a country that honored the rights of the previous sovereignties, the boundaries of such lands are still affected by the laws of the time of those countries.

There are many different ways of granting a parcel of land in the U.S., and as a result, there are different strengths of land boundaries. In a very general sense, one can place a strength based on age. If lands were allocated at a certain date, then lands conveyed later would be subject to the senior boundary, the one already in existence. Senior rights, as well as junior rights, are determined by land surveyors when retracing original boundaries.

If a tract of land is sold by a landowner, then it passes out of his or her ownership. If the next tract of land he or she sells overlaps this tract, then only the unsold portion is technically conveyed to the second owner.

The purpose of this book is not to teach people how to attempt to survey their own boundaries or determine their own property rights. This can truly be disastrous. This act can lead to the well-trod concept of spending a dollar to save a dime, although with far greater financial losses, of course.

Most landowners who hire a land surveyor do so out of necessity. Either they are purchasing land in a state that requires the parcel to be surveyed, or they have a neighbor whom they feel is encroaching in some way on their land. They have to have the land surveyed, they don't understand how this is accomplished, and likely don't understand what they will be receiving for a fee that likely is thousands of dollars.

This cost forces them to select a surveyor based on price, which allows the laws of supply and demand to come into play, forcing the professional land surveyor to try to get the job done in the least amount of time as possible.

As a result, today's surveyors don't have time to research title all the way back to its inception. Most landowners I have worked with over the years consistently believe the fee for a land survey is too expensive. However, most don't realize licensed land surveyors, who likely have the same levels of education and experience as a licensed engineer or attorney, are only able to carve out a middle-income salary from that high fee.

Many landowners don't realize the surveyor spends three

times the hours in the office than in the field and is required to pay high insurance fees due to the liability involved in determining or retracing boundaries. Many surveyors spend their own time "off the clock" conducting additional research, and on the phone or in meetings, counseling their clients in what they are actually receiving by hiring the services of a land surveyor.

The first element for a landowner to understand lies in what they receive by having their property boundary surveyed. Let's begin with a couple of key quotes from the experts:

The original surveyor creates the boundaries of a parcel through actions and words. Once an original boundary is created and described, that description remains in effect forever, legally. According to federal statutes as well as common case law, those lines remain fixed in perpetuity, from the time when the first property rights are conveyed in reliance on the lines and corners described. The surveyor is also the person who retraces the boundaries created originally and creates new evidence for future surveyors to search for.

However:

The surveyor must make the distinction between a boundary line and a property line. Boundary lines between parcels are created in several ways, yet until written documents or legal principles attach, property lines are nonexistent. In theory, a boundary line remains fixed forever where it was located initially, but a property line may change by legal principles, including estoppel, agreement, adverse possession, or riparian rights.

Brown's Boundary Control and Legal Principles, Fifth Edition

Simple, right? Well, maybe not. The important point to take from these statements is that the land surveyor can create boundaries by preparing documentation that corresponds to the appropriate laws. These boundary lines are defined through written mathematical descriptions and maps and recorded in the county the land resides in. However, the property line, or line to which a landowner has rights to, may change by the methods described above: estoppel, agreement, adverse possession, or riparian changes.

Each of these terms will be explored in more depth, but the idea is that allowing others to use the lands within the envelope of your original boundary may give them rights to these areas, as is the case in the estoppel preclusion of law, an agreement, or adverse possession. Riparian changes occur along waterways, either due to changes in the waterway, or changes in the designation or classification of the waterway.

For now, one can begin to see how an original surveyed boundary may be separate from a property or ownership line.

DETERMINING A BOUNDARY

When a land surveyor is hired to delineate a land boundary or easement, he performs title and survey records research in the county in which the land sits. Sometimes, even this can become complicated, as county lines may change over time. If, over time, new counties are created by splitting up larger counties, the records for the new county may reside in the older county courthouse, the one in which the land was originally created.

See the example on the following page:

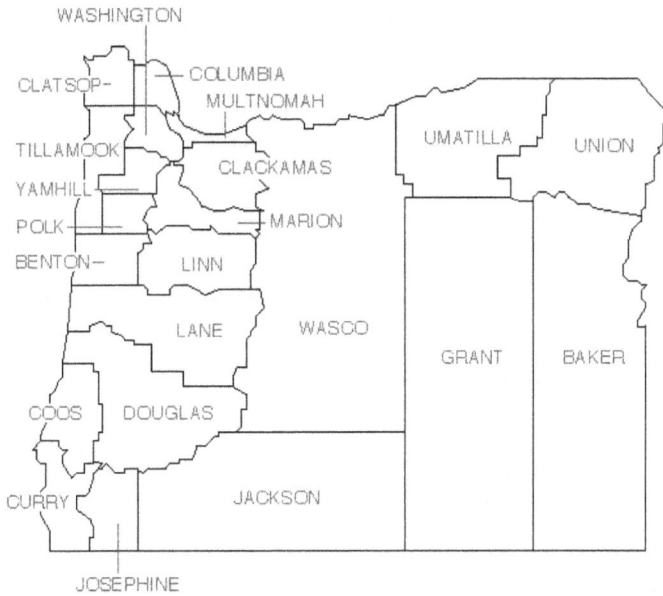

Oregon County Boundaries in 1865

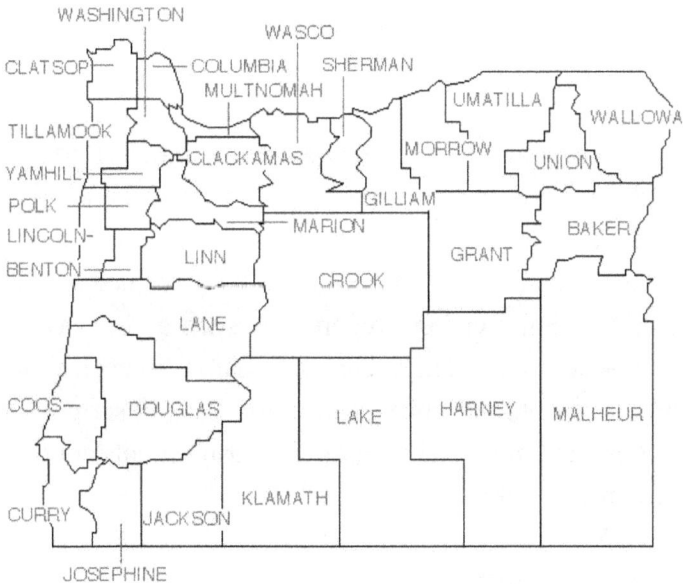

Oregon County Boundaries in 1893

So, if your land boundary was created in the central section of Jackson County (in the southern part of the state)

> **Interesting Tidbit**
>
> Many have heard of the word **Terminus** as describing the end of a line. Terminus was actually the name of the roman god of boundaries.

in 1875, then currently your land now resides in Klamath County. However, the original records for this parcel may lie in the Jackson County Courthouse.

The county courthouse is the home to the deeds that define the creation and transfers of title in land. Deeds contain not only nomenclature describing what it being sold, but also include what is called a legal description, which defines the boundary of the land. This description can be in many different forms, but this is one device a land surveyor either writes to define a new parcel of land, or retraces to delineate on the ground an existing boundary.

Some parcels are created simultaneously by dividing a large tract into many smaller ones, sometimes referred to as a land subdivision. In some instances, the subdivision map is the actual document that when recorded creates new parcels of land. If the land is sold in the future, it may be described as "Lot 2 of Happy Acres Subdivision", recorded in such-and-such county in such-and-such state. The subdivision names in each county are required to be unique. In this case, the legal description of the lot is contained in the mathematical measurements contained on the face of this map.

LEGAL DESCRIPTIONS

In the United States, there are two basic systems of

describing land: Metes and Bounds, and the Public Land Survey System. The former system is familiar to most landowners, and its name really describes two different methods of describing land which are often combined. Metes is a method of mathematically describing land controlled by courses, bearings and distances, called out along the boundary.

For example, a description might call from its point of beginning North 45° East for 200.00 feet, then South 45° East for 150.00 feet and so on, marching around the perimeter of the parcel until arriving back at the point of beginning.

A bounds description, on the other hand, simply calls out bounding features around a parcel. For example, a parcel might be described as a parcel of land, bound by the Running River on the north, the Old Town Canal on the east, County Road 345 on the south, and John Doe's farm on the west.

In a bounds survey, all the neighboring bounding elements must be surveyed to define the parcel.

Many times, metes and bounds methodology is used in describing a parcel of land. An example of a line in this type of description may read like: North 45° East along the Running River for 200.00 feet. In this instance, the Running River controls the course.

In a metes and bounds description, a monument might be called out at the end of each course, such as North 45° East 200.00 feet along the Running River to a manmade monument, such as an iron pipe driven in the ground, or to a natural monument, such as a large oak tree. When a monument is called out in a legal description, typically it controls the boundary over the course, as long as it is clearly determined to be the actual monument called out in the original description.

Highways and utility easements are often described

with a special type of metes and bounds description called a strip description. However, rather than a closed figure, a line is described. This type of description will likely also have verbiage describing the strip, such as a strip of land, 100 feet in width, lying 50 feet on each side of the following described line.

Sometimes, over many years, different surveyors determine different ideas of where a certain point may lay. One could possibly find two, three, or more monuments in an area of a corner. This is dangerous, as a landowner may think one of the monuments is the corner, when in actuality it is another, or even none at all.

In England, a process entitled *beating the bounds* was used as an ancient form of perpetuating knowledge, that of passing down information from the elders to the children of a village. In this instance, the elders who knew the locations of the land boundaries would take the young to these points and give them a memorable experience so they would always remember the location.

Interesting Tidbit

In England, village elders would pass down knowledge of boundaries through *beating the bounds*. They would show their children a corner and then give them a memorable, often painful, experience so they would always remember the location.

Wringing fingers and bouncing children on their head but were two of the ways the location was set firmly in the minds of the young.

It is the land surveyor's job to use these descriptions, as well as previous surveys and other evidence to establish or retrace the boundary of your land (no head bouncing necessary).

Prior to the mid-1780s, lands of the U.S. were typically described using metes and bounds. Our founding fathers, realizing the vast tracts of land needing to be surveyed and described in the future, began planning for a more efficient system.

In 1784, a committee headed by Thomas Jefferson proposed breaking away from metes and bounds. His proposal entailed utilizing a base-ten system, subdividing the lands into squares of 10 geographical miles each. The country apparently wasn't ready for the metric system, having its roots set deeply into the ancient metes and bounds system, and thus his proposal didn't see light.

Interesting Tidbit

In 1784, a committee headed by Thomas Jefferson proposed using the metric system to divide the un-surveyed lands of the US.

However, a year later the Continental Congress put into place the Land Ordinance of 1785, which became known as the The United States Rectangular Land Surveying System, today called the Public Land Survey System, or PLSS. Basically, this system was used to survey the massive remaining amounts of land in the U.S.

The diagram below illustrates the Public Domain States surveyed using the PLSS. However, be aware that metes and bounds is sometimes used in these states, as well.

MANUAL OF SURVEYING INSTRUCTIONS
The States created out of the Public Domain.
BLM Technical Bulletin 6

The Public Domain States

The PLSS consists of six-mile wide squares entitled townships. From an initial point of beginning of an area to be surveyed, lines are projected out in north-south and east-west directions, the north-south line titled the prime meridian, and the east-west line the base line. Townships are named based on their direction and distance from these lines. See the illustration below:

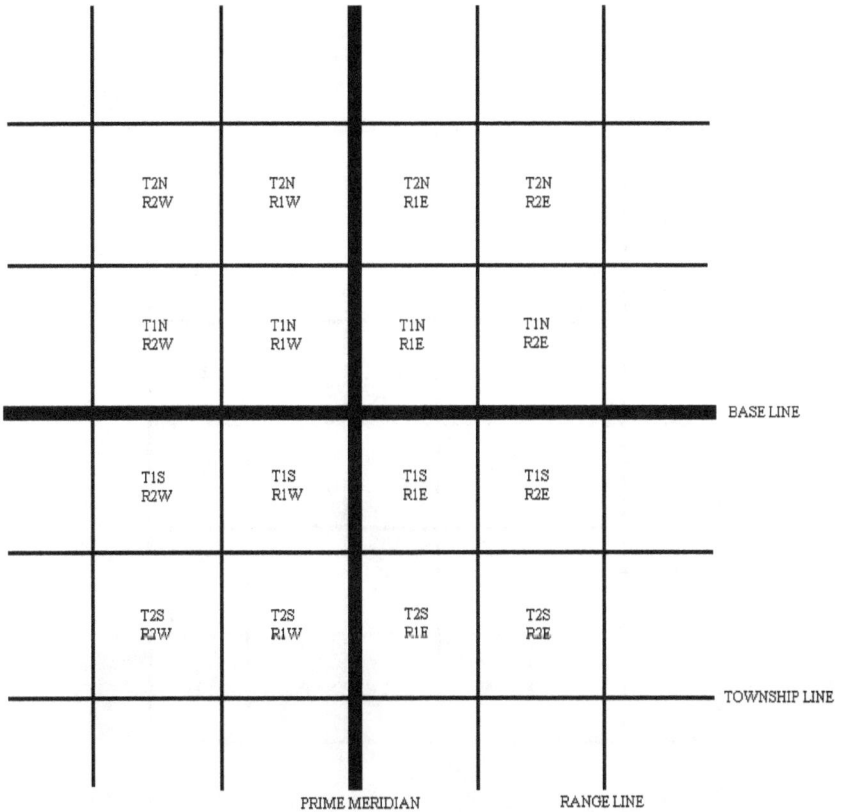

T2N R2W	T2N R1W	T2N R1E	T2N R2E
T1N R2W	T1N R1W	T1N R1E	T1N R2E
T1S R2W	T1S R1W	T1S R1E	T1S R2E
T2S R2W	T2S R1W	T2S R1E	T2S R2E

BASE LINE

TOWNSHIP LINE

PRIME MERIDIAN   RANGE LINE

Typical Township Layout

One can see how straightforward the layout of townships are arranged—property in the upper left corner of the diagram would be part of Township 2 North, Range 2 West of the Prime Meridian. Meridians are typically named; in Oregon, the prime meridian is named the Willamette Meridian.

Though the numbering system has changed over the years, currently it looks like this:

TYPICAL TOWNSHIP OF 36 SECTIONS
EACH SECTION BEING 1 MILE SQUARE

RANGE LINE

TOWNSHIP LINE

6	5	4	3	2	1
7	8	9	10	11	12
18	17	16	15	14	13
19	20	21	22	23	24
30	29	28	27	26	25
31	32	33	34	35	36

Subsequently, each section is further divided into aliquot parts. A landowner may have title to numerous sections, or to a fractional part of a section. While this type of division wasn't always followed, it is a logical way to break down large tracts of land.

An owner could simply convey the Northeast One-Quarter of Section One, Township 2 North, Range 2 West of the Willamette Meridian to a buyer and have essentially accurately described a parcel. One weakness, however, as opposed to metes and bounds, is the lack of flexibility when a seller wishes to convey a certain finite area with tricky geometric boundaries, like an area between a river and a road. To allow for this, the PLSS allows for land to be conveyed by metes and bounds. The PLSS also offers local government agencies, such as county governments, the ability to narrow down a parcel's location. A parcel's land description may begin with "A parcel of land in the Northeast One Quarter of Section One, Township 2 North, Range 2 West of the Willamette Meridian, in Crook County, Oregon, being further described as commencing at a point." A metes and bounds description would then follow.

A key element of the PLSS is that it was understood at the beginning that surveyors could never lay out perfectly square miles. Thus, it was determined by the Government Land Office, or the GLO, (now the Bureau of Land Management, or BLM) that wherever the original survey placed the corner of the township and subsequent sections corners they, once accepted by the GLO, would be the legal corners, even if the monument placement was off by many feet.

A buyer needs to understand that just because

Protection Tip

The original PLSS surveys often had large discrepancies along the edge of Townships. These edges were considered remainders, and while a person might believe they are buying a 20 acre parcel, the actual area post survey may vary substantially. A buyer should verify the actual acreage they are attaining in these areas.

they purchased a certain aliquot part of an original section, or in other words, a certain portion of an original section, that the area they purchased may not be exactly one half of 640 acres (1/2 of a section), or 40 acres (1/16 of a section), or 2.5 acres (1/256 of a section).

Typically, surveys of township boundaries happened first, and then section lines were surveyed after. When the surveys would intersect the outer township boundaries, oftentimes errors in distance would have accumulated. That error was typically left in the outer perimeter of the township, usually along the northerly and westerly edges. A buyer should be aware if purchasing in these areas to be wary of the actual acreage they are purchasing.

Metes and bounds and the PLSS allowed sellers the ability to accurately describe and then convey tracts of land. In a perfect world, these described lines would be absolute, but we all know it's not a perfect world. Let's now take a look at how over time property lines, or the lines that we actually hold ownership to, can change. As a buyer or owner, these are the lines that truly matter.

Boundaries Along Waterways

The legal term for waterway boundaries along rivers and streams is riparian boundary, and is one of the more complex boundary types to determine. Ripa is Latin for "river bank." The legal term for tidal water boundaries, or waterway boundaries influenced by the ocean

> **Information Tip**
>
> The word describing boundaries along rivers and streams is riparian while the word for describing boundaries along oceans is littoral.

tides is littoral, which comes from the Latin word litus, or "seashore."

We will go through some very general conditions of boundaries along waterways, but keep in mind, each individual state is different and one should always consult with a local qualified surveyor about their particular boundary.

There are two major differences in boundaries along rivers and streams. An adjoining landowner to such bodies either owns to the thread, or center of the stream, or they own to the river's edge. Whether one owns to the edge of the stream or to the center depends on whether the stream is considered navigable or non-navigable.

There are many definitions as to what constitutes navigability. Older English law considered waters navigable that were influenced by the ebb and flow of the sea. However, in the U.S., there are many larger rivers and inland waterways, so our definition is a bit more developed. Here, it is usually defined that if the river can be used and traveled for commerce, then it is considered navigable.

This is a touchy subject, and again, an adjoining owner must verify with the appropriate government agency whether a river or stream is considered a navigable or non-navigable waterway.

Many times legal descriptions just call to the river or stream, without defining whether it's the center or the edge of the body, and a surveyor is required to determine the stream's navigability in order to locate the boundary.

Basically, if a waterway is navigable, then the adjoining owner owns to the edge of the waterway, usually defined as the ordinary high water mark, as evident by the vegetation line alongside the body. However, this is sometimes complicated to determine, as flooding or soil types may make this line difficult to ascertain. One should also note that in some states this boundary may be the low water

Information Tip

Whether a landowner owns to the middle of a river or the edge is a question of the streams navigability.

mark. However, the public still has an interest or easement to the high water mark which is entitled the public trust.

If a waterway is considered non-navigable, then the adjoining owner owns to the center or thread of the stream. The thread is not the low point of the stream (the thalweg), but rather a line centered and perpendicular to the controlling side lines, such as the high water mark. See the illustration below to clarify.

ILLUSTRATION OF THREAD VS THALWEG

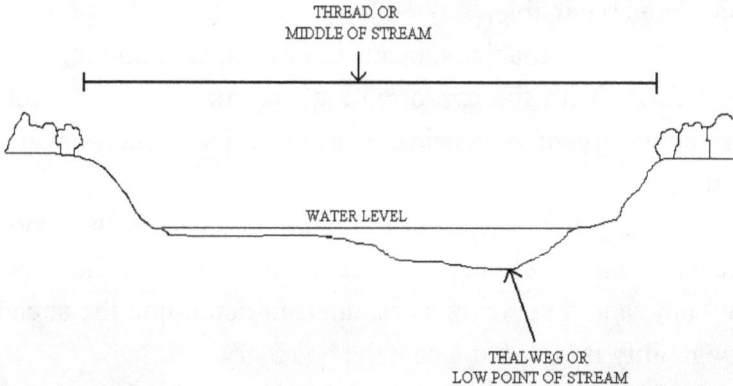

THREAD OR
MIDDLE OF STREAM

WATER LEVEL

THALWEG OR
LOW POINT OF STREAM

There are pros and cons to either owning to the center of a waterway or to the edge. For example, owning to the edge may be preferable when it comes to paying property taxes, as you may own less area, but owning to the center may be important to attain enough acreage to possibly subdivide your land.

There are many possible situations which arise in water boundaries, as in lands adjoining a man-made reservoir. Typically, if the stream prior to the reservoir was non-navigable, the adjoining owners still own to this now theoretical line that existed in the center of the stream before the lake.

However, if it was a navigable river, then the adjoining owner owns to the edge of the river where it existed prior to the lake. That is, unless the agency who created the reservoir purchased the land prior and then, of course, the boundary is as described in the new deed and lies with the purchaser.

But what if a lake is natural and non-navigable? If the body of water is round in shape, it is typically divided in a pie method, with lines projecting from the edge of the lake toward a center point. However, if the lake in long in shape, lines project from the edge and perpendicular to the thread or centerline. Still other means may be decided on by the courts and then determined in location by a land surveyor.

Littoral Boundaries

Tidal boundaries are very complex and I will only make a few very general points. Tidelands are considered the areas between high and low tides and are owned by the state. In tidal waters, again, the adjoining owner owns to a certain line alongside the body of water. This mark is determined over a significant epoch of time after analyzing the water elevation after celestial bodies have completed certain cycles, typically over an 18.6 year epoch.

Nature's Boundaries

The ownership lines along any waterway can change in many ways due to the forces of nature. In a general sense, the slow changes that happen over time will change the boundary line along a waterway. However, sudden changes from flooding, or possibly a change in the route of a river due to breaking through a bank, does not necessarily change the previous boundary line.

> **Protection Tip**
>
> Determining water boundaries is a discipline within a discipline. Do your research before selecting a land surveyor to determine a water boundary.

Just a word of caution: even land surveyors with years of education and experience are extremely careful when working along waterways. Within the profession there are those who are considered practiced in water boundaries, and there are those who are not. It pays to verify experience. However, the more you know about the rules that govern waterways, the more you can both benefit from and protect the inherent rights that come with your title.

Land Surveys

Land surveyors spend many years gaining the education and experience to properly interpret evidence to correctly create and retrace legal documents. They apply these skills carefully using all the identifiable evidence, including deeds, survey maps, and evidence collected in the field, such as survey monuments, the historical knowledge of landowners, etc.

At the completion of this in-depth study, the surveyor identifies the boundary of the parcel of land on the ground. Found survey monuments are accepted or rejected, new monuments are sometimes set, lines are marked with survey stakes in the field, and a record of survey is filed with the local county surveyor's office, who in turn sends a copy to other county departments.

So that's it, right? Have your property surveyed and the results are where your property lines lie. Maybe. Maybe not. There is a bit more to it than that.:

Many times, a neighbor approaches you stating an intention to tear down and replace a fence, remove a tree, or any number of things. At this point, you may decide to pay for a survey prior to giving your permission to remove or modify the tree, fence, etc.

In locating a land surveyor, you will likely check the phone book or Internet, or maybe visit your local county surveyor's office, all to determine who you should select to survey your land. The county surveyor's office is an excellent resource when selecting a land surveyor. Your county surveyor checks the work of the land surveyors working in your area and will likely have valuable insights and recommendations.

> **Protection Tip**
>
> When hiring a land surveyor, it's a good idea to call the county surveyor. County surveyors check the work of the local land surveyors and should be able to make a recommendation.

After checking around, you may procure a few price quotes and finally select a licensed land surveyor. Within a few weeks or sometimes months, the surveyor sets monuments and survey stakes marking the boundary described in your deed description, and, lo and behold, that tree your neighbor was going to cut is on your side of the fence.

Then, the plot thickens. Your neighbor claims the previous owner of his property planted the tree and a few others on his own property so he would know where his property lines were. His real estate agent makes the same claim. Judging by the size of the tree, it's at least 20 years old, he claims, and he has been mowing the weeds up to the tree line for the 12 years he's been your neighbor.

You hesitate after hearing your neighbor's claim, realizing someone once mentioned to you a law concerning gaining ownership of land based on usage. You get a slightly sick feeling in your gut, realizing you just spent a few thousand dollars on a survey that may be, if not irrelevant, at least only one step in a much longer process. You consider your options, wondering what to do next. Finally, you start to wonder if the tree is really worth the trouble, considering the cost of an attorney.

> **Protection Tip**
>
> Always ask this question of your land surveyor "Do you have any concerns as to the possibility of adverse possession or easements acquired by usage on my property?"

This is one of many situations landowners find themselves in on a daily basis. You may be beginning to see that while a survey can define the boundary of the land conveyed to you on paper, there may be more elements to consider.

Boundaries to Property Lines

Just about everyone who has owned land for a period of years has had situations like the one above run through their mind (or reality). The key to keeping your land and all your rights is to act before a problem arises. As a landowner, you should know what a surveyor really does, and what the results of a survey really mean.

Simply put, a surveyor locates the boundary line described in your deed and identifies encroachments or possible discrepancies between the boundary described in your deed and possession lines on the ground. This very concept is under duress in the surveying community because some experts advocate that the surveyor's job as an educated professional should go beyond merely locating a legal description, taking on the responsibility of determining property lines.

At a minimum, as professionals, land surveyors should be able to communicate to their clients how to move forward if a problem arises. Understanding this, you can know what to expect from a survey and with a little more study, can determine a sound way to move forward to protect your interests.

Technology's Affect on Boundaries

So why don't land surveyors just use GPS to find property corners? To understand why GPS cannot determine boundaries, one needs to take a look at what controls a boundary. A property's legal description begins from a survey monument and then is described either through metes and bounds or the PLSS. Either way, the boundary is

> **Information Tip**
>
> GPS is only a system of measurement. It cannot be used to determine the location of land boundaries by itself. Only a land surveyor's investigation of land records and the utilization of the appurtenant laws, combined with field evidence can determine land boundaries.

controlled by survey monuments on the ground—millions of them.

Thus, one can see, the only way to use GPS for boundaries is to actually survey all the boundary controls with GPS. If this is done correctly, and the GPS survey is connected to GPS monuments that will always be perpetuated, then GPS can be used to determine what is considered geodetic coordinates on the boundary corners.

Once these geodetic coordinates, or accurate positions within the Global Positioning System, are established, theoretically, a surveyor can relocate and even reset survey monuments.

Our Changing Property Lines

In the next chapter, we'll take a look at some of the ways boundaries and property lines can change over the years and how you, the landowner, can prevent this.

CHAPTER 5 – KEY POINTS

✓ The original surveyor creates the boundaries of a parcel through actions and words. Once an original boundary is created and described, that description remains in effect forever, legally. According to federal statutes as well as common case law, those lines remain fixed in perpetuity, from the time when the first property rights are conveyed in reliance on the lines and corners described. The surveyor is also the person who retraces the boundaries created originally and creates new evidence for future surveyors to search for.

✓ The surveyor must make the distinction between a boundary line and a property line. Boundary lines between parcels are created in several ways, yet until written documents or legal principles attach, property lines are nonexistent. In theory, a boundary line remains fixed forever where it was located initially, but a property line may change by legal principles, including estoppel, agreement, adverse possession, or riparian rights.

✓ Land surveyors write land descriptions which are made a part of a deed and allow the parcel to be located on the ground now and in the future.

✓ In 1785, the Continental Congress put into place the Land Ordinance of 1785, which became known as the The United States Rectangular Land Surveying System, today called the Public Land Survey System or PLSS. For the most part, this system was used to survey the massive remaining amounts of land in the US.

✓ Boundaries along rivers and streams are described as riparian while the word for describing boundaries along oceans is littoral.

✓ Whether a landowner owns to the middle of a river or the edge is a question of the streams navigability.

✓ Determining water boundaries is a discipline within a discipline. Do your research before selecting a land surveyor to determine a water boundary.

6

Adverse Possession

All the territorial possessions of all the political establishments in the earth—including American, of course—consist of pilferings from other people's wash. No tribe, howsoever insignificant, and no nation, howsoever mighty occupies a foot of land that was not stolen.
Mark Twain

Adverse Possession
The use or enjoyment of real property with a claim of right when that use or enjoyment is continuous, exclusive, hostile, open, and notorious.
Black's Law Dictionary, Eighth Edition

At one time or another, most landowners have heard about the concept of losing some land to a neighbor simply because their neighbor possessed and used the land for a certain period of time. I myself have nearly fallen prey to this law, but having knowledge of how the law works and the list of requirements to adversely possess, I was able to negate any claim my neighbor might have.

The matter began during the closing of a 10-acre parcel I had recently made an offer to purchase. One day, while visiting the parcel to scope out a home site, I noticed the neighbor's truck parked across the property line. Prior to making an offer, I had already perused the legal description and the neighboring parcels legal descriptions and determined a survey had been performed in the '70s that coincided with the deeds to mark not only my boundary, but also the boundaries of the properties on all sides.

This was a very good sign, as the survey and legal descriptions all matched exactly without overlaps or gaps; thus, I didn't suspect any ambiguity in the boundaries around the parcel. I had located the survey monuments and knew where the lines were on the ground, however, it was forestland and there were no fences, hedges, or other definite occupation lines.

It became apparent the neighbor was accustomed to parking across the line. While our driveways were separated by a good 30 feet, his driveway came very close to the line as it contoured up toward his

---

Information Tip

It is important to build repore with a neighbor before breaching a possible property rights issue. First and foremost, take the time to handle things in a neighborly fashion.

---

home. Outside his driveway, where it neared the boundary, was his selected parking place. I took a few minutes and walked along the property line, and on closer inspection, noticed he had piled some building materials in the bushes across the line as well, which appeared to have been grown over by vegetation some years ago.

The situation could have been handled many ways, but my experience in land surveying over the previous two decades suggests building bonds first. It is crucial to ease tension and raise the confidence level in a landowner that you are a moral and honest person. When it comes to land, people are generally on guard so it pays to take your time and build rapport. This will encourage most to be open and honest with you in return.

To begin the process of communication, I visited the site often in the evenings after work, always keeping an eye out for my neighbor, rather than simply banging on his door and confronting him on his doorstep. When I finally caught him outside, I took the time to chat about my plans to build a home for my family, and also explained that because I had a young child, one of my first tasks would be to fence the lower section of the property. I let him show me the property survey monument between the driveways and as we both looked up the line, I waited for him to bring up the fact that his possessions were encroaching.

After some beating around the bush, I realized the topic wasn't going to surface. So, I politely mentioned that once I was in possession of the land and getting the fence underway that I would like him to clean up his crap. I told him not to hurry, of course, and that I would be glad to help. It was then in that moment that any chances of him adversely possessing the land ended: This is because, very simply, he mentioned that the existing owner had given him permission to park his truck across the property line.

By admitting he was acting under the owner's permission, he no longer met one of the requirements for adverse possession, which is to hold the property in a hostile manner, essentially one that states to the world that "this is my land."

Later, I also spoke with the owner of the parcel I was buying; he confirmed that he had given the neighbor permission. I also mentioned to the owner that I would like him to handle the matter prior to closing. And while I didn't have a contingency in my offer that stated he

---

Protection Tip

The best way to defend against an adverse possessor is to give them permission to use your land. By agreeing to your permission, the possessor is admitting they do not own the land in question. It is best to get this permission in writing and consult your attorney about the best approach to take in your state.

---

needed to take care of this problem, I had plenty of other ways to back out of the deal if I needed to. This situation was indeed handled prior to closing, which is ideal. However, many times a landowner doesn't realize there is a possible claim until after they own the property.

The Use or Enjoyment of Real Property

Black's Law Dictionary's definition of adverse possession begins with "the use and enjoyment of real property" under certain conditions. Basically, the property has to be in use by the possessing party. He must show evidence of treating the property as his own by having some tangible occupation of the land area. Not only does the person have to be in actual possession of the land, but also then meet the following requirements:

The Continuous Adverse Use Principle

For a statutory period, the party must continuously use the land area. In other words, the state you live in sets the time requirement for adverse possession claims. Some states also require that taxes have been paid on the subject property for the statutory period. For the use to be continuous, a party can't break the use, and then restart the use again. However, use can pass from one owner to the next, as long as it is continuous. This is the principle of tacking and may allow the continuous use time period of the previous owner to essentially be tacked on to the new owner's time period. However, if any time period exists between ownerships, there is no continuity.

The Exclusive Use Principle

This simply means there must be a sole occupant claiming the property. If two neighbors park along a strip of land owned by another, the use is not exclusive. There may be a prescriptive easement established, but a neighbor can't gain ownership of the land when multiple parties are using an area.

The Hostile Use Principle

This condition is different from state to state. The most common principle is known as the Connecticut Rule, which requires simple occupation of the land. The occupant doesn't have to be aware that they are using someone else's land. A few states require awareness, and a few others require unawareness. One should consult with a land use attorney to determine the law in their state.

The Open and Notorious Use Principle

This particular type of use requires the adverse possessor to somehow display to the community and the owner that they possess the land. This requires evidencing the fact, possibly by building a fence, a shed, planting trees or bushes, and then maintaining them. The idea is that the owner can see someone is occupying the area in question.

Proof of Paying Taxes

It should be noted that a handful of states require proof of paying taxes on the land in question to achieve title through adverse possession. Also, in some states, proof of paying taxes may reduce the statutory time requirement.

Statutory Time Requirement

Each state has time requirements for adverse possession. All the above uses have to be met for a certain number of years, and as mentioned above, tacking may occur, so long as the use is continuous. On the following page I have listed the time requirements for each individual state.

ADVERSE POSSESSION – STATUTORY TIME REQUIREMENTS (IN YEARS)

ALABAMA	10	KENTUCKY	15	NORTH DAKOTA	20
ALASKA	10	LOUISIANA	30	OHIO	21
ARIZONA	10	MAINE	20	OKLAHOMA	15
ARKANSAS	7	MARYLAND	20	OREGON	10
CALIFORNIA	5	MASSACHUSETTS	20	PENNSYLVANIA	21
COLORADO	18	MICHIGAN	15	RHODE ISLAND	10
CONNECTICUT	15	MINNESOTA	15	SOUTH CAROLINA	10
DELAWARE	20	MISSISSIPPI	10	SOUTH DAKOTA	20
D. C.	15	MISSOURI	10	TENNESSEE	7
FLORIDA	7	MONTANA	5	TEXAS	10
GEORGIA	20	NEBRASKA	10	UTAH	7
HAWAII	20	NEVADA	15	VERMONT	15
IDAHO	20	NEW HAMPSHIRE	20	VIRGINIA	15
ILLINOIS	20	NEW JERSEY	30	WASHINGTON	10
INDIANA	10	NEW MEXICO	10	WEST VIRGINIA	10
IOWA	10	NEW YORK	10	WISCONSIN	20
KANSAS	15	NORTH CAROLINA	20	WYOMING	10

There are additional requirements that when met can reduce the time required for an adverse possession case, such as proof of paying taxes on the subject area. One should always consult their land use attorney in these matters.

A Last Alternative

No matter what, trying to recover a strip that has been used by someone else for many years will likely be ugly. Attorney fees, land surveyor fees, possible property damage, and court costs are likely some things you don't want to get involved in if you can avoid it.

Across the board, I hear from people who went to court over issues like adverse possession that they wish they'd come to some resolution on their own. If granting permission doesn't work, then possibly there is another way to peacefully rectify the situation while holding onto the value of your investment. If neighbors can be made aware of how the discrepancy occurred, they will likely be more open to making things right.

For example, many times adverse possession isn't confined to one property line. Owners may have attempted to survey their property without the aid of a land surveyor. In this instance, while one neighbor may be encroaching 10 feet onto your described parcel on one side, you may likely be encroaching on the next parcel over in the same manner.

> ### Information Tip
>
> Adverse possession often promulgates across many parcels. If one can determine this common discrepancy one may be able to get a group of neighbors together to handle the situation in a logical and fair manner.

Imagine if Joe the farmer, planning his retirement, divided off three five-acre tracts off the front of his thousand-acre farm. His overall tract was already surveyed and the corners set so he takes his trusty tape measure down to his property corner and measures off the frontages of each square five-acre parcel.

Joe does a pretty good job, carefully measuring 466.69 feet down the edge of the road and setting a stake at each measurement. His property is on a slope, so by the time he gets finished, he's a bit winded, and waits till the next day to mark the side lines.

The next morning, he pulls out his trusty compass, sights from the roadway corners away from the road, and measures to the back corners. He then measures between the back corners to check his work, and lo and behold the distances check pretty well, except for one distance: the distance across the back of Lot 1.

Now Joe becomes suspicious, realizing the fence line along his outer boundary must be off. He'd measured too carefully for it to be anything else. He traipses home, bent on getting his property lines checked. But in time, or because of lack of funds, he lets it go. He builds fences between the points he set, records deeds, and thinks about how much he'll get for the lots in a few decades.

This situation is not that uncommon. In fact, something similar happened on a parcel of land neighboring my parents' house. It will become apparent that Joe made a couple of big mistakes, such as not accounting for the fact that survey measurements need to be made along a level line. He was measuring uphill, and therefore his distances came up short. Joe was also using a compass that was oriented toward magnetic north, whereas his deed said true north.

By the way, just like in electricity and plumbing, a landowner can write his own land description without any special license or training, although I have a hard time imagining anything more disastrous. Take a look at the illustration below to see what I mean:

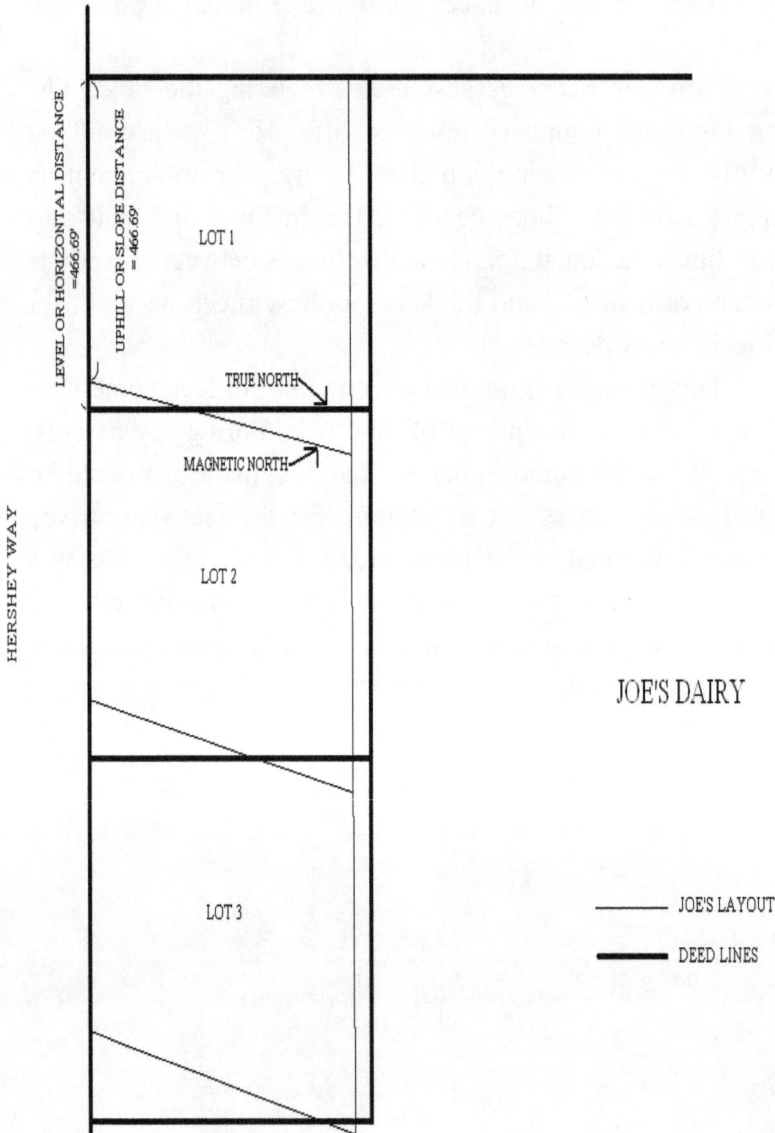

LEVEL OR HORIZONTAL DISTANCE =466.69'

UPHILL OR SLOPE DISTANCE = 466.69'

LOT 1

TRUE NORTH

MAGNETIC NORTH

HERSHEY WAY

LOT 2

JOE'S DAIRY

LOT 3

——— JOE'S LAYOUT

▬▬▬ DEED LINES

After studying the diagram, one can see why Joe's measurement across the back of Lot 1 looked a bit funny. Surveyors typically have many different learned rules and laws that govern how they retrace a land description. To see how his distances measured up the hill could be so far off, take a look at the illustration below:

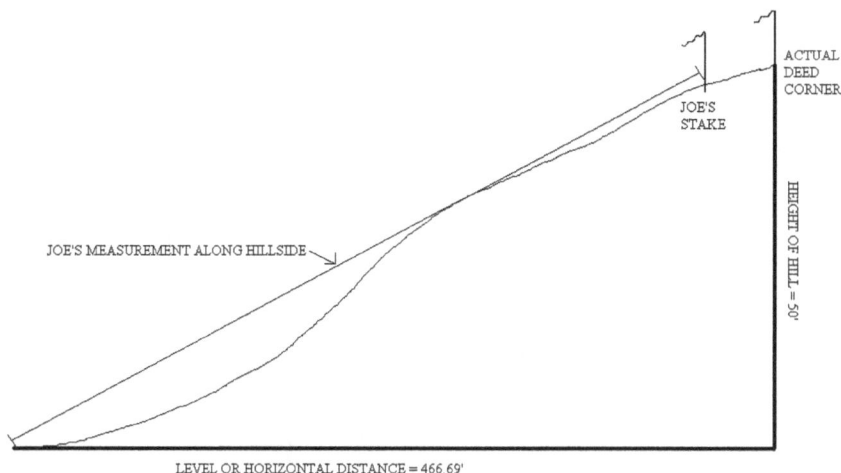

JOE'S STAKE

ACTUAL DEED CORNER

JOE'S MEASUREMENT ALONG HILLSIDE

HEIGHT OF HILL = 50'

LEVEL OR HORIZONTAL DISTANCE = 466.69'

His other big mistake was using a compass orientated to magnetic north rather than true north, which is illustrated in the side lines of Lots 1, 2, and 3. Surveyors don't just have to measure direction accurately; they also have to determine which type of direction they are using. Directions can be based on everything from solar observations, to older surveys, to large and complex mathematical models such as is used with GPS.

Poor Joe didn't have a chance.

However, this illustrates how adverse possession can happen. In this instance, it may be wise to work with several neighbors to come to some resolution. Most of the time, a neighbor is not trying to steal your land; they just believe the line is as it looks on the ground. If you and your neighbor can agree on occupation lines, there are a couple of ways to clean up the discrepancy.

Boundary Line Agreements

If you and your neighbor agree on where you like a dividing line to be, there may be a way to legalize the line through a boundary line agreement (BLA). Generally there are four legal requirements that must be met for a court of law to recognize a BLA.

1. The line must be ambiguous or uncertain, which means that by using the deed descriptions, the line must not be able to be found accurately.
2. The new line must be visually identifiable on the ground.
3. You and your neighbor must agree upon the identifiable line.
4. You both must act as if the line is truly the property line by using the area up to the line.

The later three requirements are fairly easily achieved, but it is the first that is the real kicker. To achieve this, it is best to have a qualified land surveyor attempt to locate the line, and then get his or her advice on how to proceed. A BLA may be an option, but one needs to be careful to follow the requirements

Protection Tip

To utilize a boundary line agreement or BLA to settle a property line dispute the boundary must be ambiguous or unable to be fixed by a licensed land surveyor.

so as to not have the line disputed and rejected later in court.

Books on legal advice in uncertain boundaries situations also suggest two neighbors filing Quit-Claim Deeds, giving any interest to each other on the other side of an agreed upon line such as a fence or other fixed construction. However, one must be very careful to follow not only statute law, but also local code. Agreeing on an occupation line and filing Quit-Claim Deeds may change the configuration of a property, making it narrower, or of a lower acreage than the local zoning allows. If an owner attempts later to get approval for an addition to their home, or a new driveway, or any number of things, the agency may turn them down until they make their parcel conform to zoning regulations.

Another problem that may arise is that most lien holders, i.e. your mortgage company, may likely have a clause in your title that allows them to full and immediate payment of the entire mortgage if the owner gives away any interest in the property. I will cover zoning and mortgage company requirements in later chapters on land development, but one must be aware of these requirements in settling ambiguous property lines as well.

> ### Protection Tip
>
> Your mortgage company can likely call a note due if any part of the interest in their collateral is deeded away to another party.

Many times, however, neighbors can't come to terms and agree upon the position of a property line. When a boundary line is under dispute, but a claim of adverse possession is not valid, another situation can arise. Even if all of the requirements for adverse possession are not met, but certain uses are proven, it is still possible for someone to gain a right to use the subject piece of land.

To understand the concept better, we should go back to our analogy that title to land is really ownership of a whole bundle of property rights, the symbol once again the bundle of sticks tied together by the belt of title. In this instance, you, the landowner, can lose one of these sticks to your neighbor through your neighbor's establishment of a *prescriptive easement.*

CHAPTER 6 – KEY POINTS

✓ Adverse Possession is the use or enjoyment of real property with a claim of right when that use or enjoyment is continuous, exclusive, hostile, open and notorious.

✓ Each state has time requirements for Adverse Possession and may also require proof of the paying of taxes by the possessor.

✓ The best way to defend against an adverse possessor is to give permission to use your land. By agreeing to your permission, the possessor is admitting they do not own the land in question. It is best to get this permission in writing and consult your attorney about the best approach to take in your state.

✓ If you and your neighbor agree on where you like a dividing line to be, there may be a way to legalize the line through a boundary line agreement (BLA). However, there are legal requirements that must be met for a court of law to recognize a BLA.

✓ Your mortgage company can likely call a note due if any part of the interest in their collateral is deeded away to another party.

7

Intentional and Unintentional Easements

An easement is simply an interest or right to use land owned by someone else. The easement is for a specific use or uses and does not give the easement holder, which is referred to as the *dominant estate*, the right to make improvements to, take away from, or, of course, sell the land. However, the easement may and probably will, unless written otherwise, pass on to the next owner.

Typically, an easement will be written to a party, and his heirs and assigns, or the next title holders. Holding an easement on someone else's land is holding one of their sticks from their bundle of property rights and vice versa.

Common types of easements are right-of-way easements for roads or railways; utility easements for utility companies to cross your land with their lines; ingress egress easements for access to and from a parcel; light and air easements, or restrictions from constructing anything that would prevent light or air from reaching a dominant estate; and water easements for irrigation, wells, etc.

The idea of easements in general is a pretty simple one. However, as a landowner, there are a couple of things to watch out for that can be devastating to your investment.

The first is when after a cursory review of the title report, the buyer doesn't realize the exact property right and location a dominant estate has on your soon-to-be parcel. This often happens when purchasing homes that are a few or more years old. On newly subdivided lands, sticky easements and encumbrances in the existing larger tract are typically cleaned up by the land developer prior to subdividing.

With older lots, and especially rural properties, there is often a list of existing easements in the title report, and each should be researched thoroughly prior to purchase. And, from experience, I know that title and real estate professionals can be a little anxious to close a deal, and oftentimes give the buyer a bit of a false sense of security. In an investment so large as purchasing land and home, it pays to be extra cautious.

> **Protection Tip**
>
> Title officers, real estate brokers and mortgage brokers can be anxious to close a deal, and may give you, the buyer, a false sense of security. In an investment so large as purchasing land and home, it pays to be more cautious than you are likely used to.

Even as a licensed land surveyor, I've fallen prey to this mistake, believing an irrigation easement on an investment parcel of land I was buying was for an open irrigation ditch at the front of the property. Later, when seeking to gain approval to develop, I discovered the easement was for a pipeline crossing the property to benefit a neighbor. Had this easement been underneath a future home site, I could have been in serious trouble.

Not being aware of easement locations can be a very costly mistake, making it all the more important as a buyer to have a professional identify and locate all the easements shown in a title report prior to purchase.

The second type of easement that can be troublesome is the one that you as the buyer or owner don't know about because it didn't show up in your title report. In fact, it may not be written down at all. Easements by necessity fall into this category. If it is absolutely necessary for someone to cross your land for access to their land, the law will often allow that access, and you can't do anything to stop them.

Another easement to watch out for is the one that didn't make it into the title report because it simply didn't get caught in the title search. Title companies have certain methods they follow in doing their research, and at times, only go back a certain number of years to check for encumbrances, so it always pays to have the full chain of title researched in the county records when purchasing land.

> ### Protection Tip
>
> If it is necessary for someone to cross your land to access their own the courts will usually grant an easement for this access, an easement of necessity.

And there is one additional type of easement that is most sure not to make it in a typical title report, as we touched on in the previous chapter.

Similar to adverse possession, a party can gain what is known as a prescriptive easement by using a part of your land, and the list of usage requirements isn't as stiff as it is for adverse possession. For a prescriptive easement, only the uses of open, adverse, and continuous apply (refer back to the section on adverse possession requirements for a description of these uses.)

Another key point is that multiple parties can gain a prescriptive easement from use in this manner, as is the case when a private road or irrigation ditch crosses your property.

The best defense against prescriptive easements, as in adverse possession, is permission of the owner. All an owner has to do is allow a party permission to use the land to negate a prescriptive easement claim, and the neighbor acknowledge this allowance, which is always best done in writing. In some instances, even

> **Protection Tip**
>
> The best defense against a prescriptive easement is through granting the other party permission for the use.

friendship can imply permission. If you are on friendly terms with your neighbor then it appears likely you would allow him to use your land.

The important thing is to be proactive. Many times easements can be headed off before they fully ripen, especially if the other party doesn't become suspicious he or she is going to lose the right to the usage. Then, when the property sells, you can end the usage.

A more difficult prescriptive easement to defend against is one used by multiple parties, such as a beach trail or private drive. In this instance, an owner may be able to provide the notice by placing signs along the road or trail. However, it is always best to get permission in writing.

Rights of Way

Many government and quasi-government agencies such as railroads and large utilities purchase or take what is entitled a right-of-way easement. In this instance, the agency owns an easement for the road and possibly utilities over a strip of land; the underlying ownership is still yours.

There are pros and cons in owning to the center of the road, just as in owning to the center of a waterway. One plus is that you may be able to use this acreage out to the centerline to achieve a large enough parcel to meet the county or city requirements to subdivide; the negative, again, is paying property taxes on land you can't use.

I once worked on an interesting survey of a property adjoining an old railroad easement that was established by an act of congress in the 1880s. The current landowner owned a narrow triangular parcel alongside the rail line. An old existing fence line ran parallel and 30 feet off the centerline of the rail.

Upon researching the deed, I traced the parcel back to its inception in a land grant from the government in the 1880s. This document described the parcel, and called out to a 60 foot-wide railroad right-of-way, 30 feet on each side of the rail line. However, I also discovered the original right-of-way map, signed by owners in the area, which showed a 200 foot right-of-way width for the railroad, 100 feet on each side of the rail.

If the railroad map was right, then the parcel would be devastated. Not only would most of my client's parcel now be within the right-of-way, but also his home as well.

Later, in court, the 60-foot width was upheld due to the discovery of proof that the original owner was occupying and using all the area outside the 60 foot strip, as it still was currently in use.

In closing, I will touch on a subject that gets most citizens up in arms on occasion, which is the possibility of the government gaining a right-of-way through a process known as *eminent domain.*

Eminent Domain

The power to take private property for public use by a state, municipality, or private person or corporation authorized to exercise functions of public character, following the payment of just compensation to the owner of that property.
The Legal Dictionary

The Fifth Amendment to the Constitution provides that private property cannot be taken for public use without just compensation.

The basics of condemnation are fairly common knowledge. When the federal, state, county, or city government requires additional right-of-way for a new or existing roadway, eminent domain may be set into motion.

Once the preliminary design is completed for a road widening, for example, the agency will send out a specialized appraiser to determine the impact to the owner's property rights and essentially appraise that value based on current market trends. They will then make an offer to purchase the land from the owner. If the owner agrees to the price, they are compensated, deeds are signed, and the project moves forward. If they don't, the agency is forced into the more expensive process of condemnation, or taking the land through the power of *eminent domain.*

For a landowner, this can be difficult to stomach. We pride ourselves in our freedom, but in these instances we realize that we really live under some clearly defined rules, most of which are deemed necessary for the public good. All of us appreciate being able to utilize streamlined roadway corridors that let us get to work on time, or possibly a parking strip between the curb and sidewalk to allow a few trees to replenish our oxygen supply, just so long as the public improvement is truly for the public's greater good, and not merely a convenience to an agency. However, this isn't always how the power of eminent domain is used.

A few years ago, CBS News reported on an eminent domain case in Lakewood, Ohio. The city of Lakewood proposed condemnation of an entire neighborhood of 55 homes, four apartment buildings, and more than a dozen businesses. For a new highway, you ask? A new water tank to account for urban growth? Nope. The city had sought out a land developer to develop high-end condos and a shopping mall. According to the report by CBS, the move would strengthen Lakewood's property tax base and generate more tax dollars for the city government.

Protection Tip

Government agencies can condemn privately owned land for the purpose of private development if they can meet certain federal and statutory requirements.

To successfully condemn the homes in the area, the city would be required to prove the homes and area were considered blighted, which in a general sense means that structures don't meet current standards. According to a citizen's quote in the report, in Lakewood, this meant a home must have three bedrooms, two bathrooms, an attached two-car garage, and central air conditioning. The neighborhood was fairly old, but in good condition. However, often times older homes only include one bathroom and detached garages.

The homeowners eventually won out, rejecting the new development. However, this isn't always the case. If an agency can make the case that a private development is for the public good, they may be able to condemn.

But, aside from the obvious, is there a high side to condemnation? There may be. In many instances, agencies know they need right-of-way for roadway widening years in advance. During the funding stages of a new project, they may simply wait for local owners to come to them with applications to improve their property.

At this they smile, and say "sure, but we will require an additional so-many feet of right-of-way across the front of your lot prior to approval." Lot by lot, parcel by parcel, the agency slowly gets their right-of-way. But if the landowner is savvy, they can gain compensation for this right-of-way when they wish. If you determine the agency needs this land, approach them about it and offer to sell it to them. By being proactive, a landowner may gain thousands of dollars at a time when they wish rather than at a time of the agency's choosing.

There are many ways to determine prior to purchasing land if easements or other rights have been granted or lost to another party. Knowing this, one route to determining the real condition of a parcel is through hiring a title officer or land surveyor to research the chain of title, such as through an ALTA ACSM Land Title Survey.

CHAPTER 7 – KEY POINTS

✓ An *easement* is simply an interest or right to use land owned by someone else. The easement is for a specific use or uses and does not give the easement holder, which is referred to as the *dominant estate*, the right to make improvements to, take away from, or, of course, sell the land. However, the easement may and probably will unless written otherwise, pass on to the next owner.

✓ Common types of easements are right-of-way easements for roads or railways; utility easements for utility companies to cross your land with their lines; ingress egress easements for access to and from a parcel; light and air easements, or restrictions from constructing anything that would prevent light or air from reaching a dominant estate; and water easements for irrigation, wells, etc.

✓ If it is necessary for someone to cross your land to access their own the courts will usually grant an easement for this access, an easement of necessity.

✓ Similar to adverse possession, a party can gain what is known as a *prescriptive easement* by using a part of your land. And the list of usage requirements isn't as stiff as it is for adverse possession. For a prescriptive easement, only the uses of open, adverse, and continuous apply.

✓ As with adverse possession, the best defense against a prescriptive easement is through granting the other party permission for the use.

✓ Eminent Domain is the power to take property for public use by a state, municipality, or private person or corporation authorized to exercise functions of public character, following the payment of just compensation to the owner of that property.

✓ Government agencies can condemn privately owned land for the purpose of private development if they can meet certain federal and statutory requirements.

8

Protection Against Acts of God

Act of God
An overwhelming, unpreventable event caused exclusively by
forces of nature, such as in earthquake, flood, or tornado. The
definition has been statutorily broadened to include all natural
phenomena that are exceptional, inevitable, and irresistible,
the effects of which could not be prevented or avoided by the
exercise of due care or foresight.
Black's Law Dictionary, Eighth Edition

It's interesting how homeowners view potential risk from acts of god. Most homeowners and/or landowners in the U.S., whether they admit it or not, are under some threat of natural disaster, from hurricanes in the southern and southeast section of the country, to tornadoes across our middle regions, to earthquakes in the southwest, to forest fires in the northwest, to flooding everywhere, we all suffer some level of liability.

Many of us look at the inhabitants of New Orleans who suffered such tremendous loss when the dikes gave way to floodwaters caused by Hurricane Katrina and wonder why they live under such risk. However, I'm fairly certain some New Orleans residents may look at the citizens of Southern California and shudder at the idea of a 6.0-plus earthquake, or look at those who live in the forests of the Pacific Northwest and cringe at the idea of living out in the forests, a.k.a. the tinderboxes of our country.

But aside from the obvious steps to safeguarding our investments, such as buying in an area not terribly prone to natural disasters, what defense do we have? The simple answer: buy the appropriate insurance. However, many of us do not have a good grip on what insurance we really need, and what the insurers actually cover under the policies they sell us. For example, many of us do not realize until it is too late that flood or earthquake damage may not be covered under our current policies.

Insurance transfers the liability of a loss from one party to another in exchange for a premium. To be successful, insurers have to be experts at calculating levels of risk, charging enough to make a profit from premiums while still compensating for damages. On the insurers' side of the fence, this is considered *the law of large numbers,* which is purely based on the laws of probability and statistics, showing that as the number of exposed units increases, the likelihood of predicting an expected result increases also.

Just by owning the right insurance, one should realize that the insurer is betting you likely won't incur

> **Information Tip**
>
> Insurance companies are in business to make money! If they issue insurance, they are betting they will make money on your policy. Take the time to purchase the insurance that best protects your investment.

damages. To get a handle on the current state of homeowner insurance, let's begin with how insurance originated in the U.S.

History of Insurance

Since one caveman clubbed another from an invading tribe for trying to steal his mate, one can say insurance existed. After all, that club was providing a certain amount of insurance in safety. (We won't delve into the premium.)

However, it was the Great Fire of London in 1666 that stimulated the first insurance office as we know it today. This tragedy, which destroyed more than 13,000 homes, resulted in one Nicholas Barbon opening an office offering insurance to the owners of structures.

In 1732, the United States' first insurance company began in Charleston, South Carolina, which also underwrote fire insurance. Twenty years later, Benjamin Franklin brought together the Philadelphia Contributionship for the Insurance of Houses from Loss by Fire. His organization began the process of educating homeowners in fire safety. The Contributionship would only offer insurance if the risk was limited, turning away all wooden structures, for they held too high a risk.

Today, homeowners with mortgages, i.e. nearly all of us, are required to hold what is entitled a homeowner's insurance policy.

What is in a standard homeowner's insurance policy?

A standard homeowner's insurance policy includes four essential types of coverage.

1. Coverage for the *structure* of your home.

2. Coverage for your *personal belongings.*

3. *Liability* protection, as in protection from being sued by someone injured on your property.

4. Additional *living expenses* in the event you are temporarily unable to live in your home because of a fire or other insured disaster.

What is typically not covered? Flood and earthquake protection, as mentioned earlier; each of these policies are purchased separately. Earthquake insurance is expensive and typically only purchased in certain areas of the country. One should speak to their insurance agency about the cost-to-benefit ratio of earthquake insurance in your local area. As for flood insurance, it pays to know the ins and outs of the system, whether buying or simply verifying coverage of your existing property.

Flood Insurance

Due to the higher likelihood of damages in certain areas, many private insurance companies will not issue flood insurance for homes along waterways. Again, insurance companies are businesses, and when the risk of payout outweighs what consumers will pay in premiums, well, selling insurance is bad business. However, the scenic and recreational value of living near water is attractive to many of us, and as a

> **Protection Tip**
>
> Flood and earthquake insurance are typically not covered in a standard homeowner's insurance policy. These are separate policies a buyer should purchase in certain areas.

result there are still vast quantities of structures that exist and that continue to be built along waterways.

To mitigate flood damage to existing homes, as well as provide protection for new ones, the federal government stepped in, implementing the Flood Disaster Protection Act in 1973. This act is administered by the Flood Emergency Management Agency, better known as FEMA. Here's an excerpt from the act:

The 1973 Act prohibits Federal agencies from providing financial assistance for acquisition or construction of buildings and certain disaster assistance in the floodplains in any community that did not participate in the NFIP by July 1,1975, or within 1 year of being identified as flood-prone.

Additionally, the 1973 Act required that Federal agencies and federally insured or regulated lenders had to require flood insurance on all grants and loans for acquisition or construction of buildings in designated Special Flood Hazard Areas (SFHAs) in communities that participate in the NFIP. This requirement is referred to as the Mandatory Flood Insurance Purchase Requirement. The SFHA is that land within the floodplain of a community subject to a 1 percent or greater chance of flooding in any given year, commonly referred to as the 100-year flood.

The 100-year flood area was determined through engineering studies of photogrammetric mapping and field surveys. Using topographical maps developed through aerial photographs, engineers performed analyses on the rivers and streams in the United States. See the example below of part of a Flood Insurance Rate Map, or FIRM:

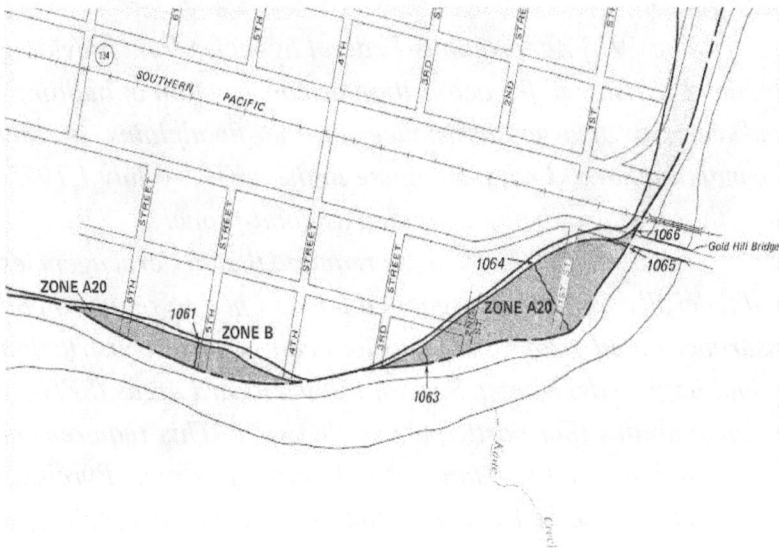

You will notice there are zone designations alongside the edge of the river. Each FIRM includes a legend to determine the definition of each zone. In this instance, Zone B indicates the 500-Year Flood Boundary, and Zone A indicates the 100-Year Flood Boundary. The numbers alongside the stream indicate the Base Flood Elevation, or BFE of the 100-Year Flood Boundary. This elevation plays a key role in determining the future elevation of structures permitted within the 100- Year Flood Boundary. More from the Flood Disaster Protection Act:

The regulatory floodway is defined as the channel of a stream plus any adjacent floodplain areas that must be kept free of encroachment so that the entire Base Flood (100-Year Flood) discharge can be conveyed with no greater than a 1.0-foot increase in the BFE.

See the example below to aid in understanding building regulations within the 100-Year Floodway:

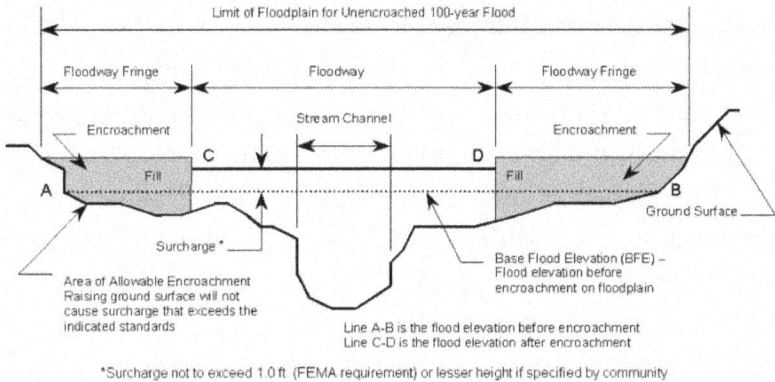

Floodplain·Encroachment·and·Floodway

The floodway includes the channel and adjacent floodplain area that is required to pass the 100-Year Flood without unduly increasing flood heights. The floodway fringe is the portion of the floodplain that contains slow moving or standing water. Development in the fringe will not normally interfere with the flow of water. Development may be allowed in the floodway fringe; however, the elevation of the buildings must be above the 100-Year-Flood elevation or the buildings must be made watertight.

Land Use Controls and Property Rights, John P. Lewis

To secure insurance, even when the floor elevation of a structure is above the BFE, a specially designed foundation may be required that will allow floodwaters to travel through the foundation area without affecting the flood plain.

Land surveyors determine whether existing buildings or future building sites are within the floodway. Sometimes it may not be discovered that a structure is in or near the floodway until an owner tries to sell or refinance their home. Bank regulatory agencies and secondary market agencies (e.g. Fannie Mae and Freddie Mac) are responsible for enforcing the law by requiring borrowers to obtain flood insurance for the extent of their loans.

Also, to obtain disaster relief, local government agencies are required to adopt floodplain management practices. Each controlling agency must participate in the National Flood Insurance Program and accept FEMA's FIRM mapping in their subject areas.

Local governments may also provide local engineering studies in areas where they believe changes have occurred in the floodway, or when seeking a more accurate floodway model than what the original studies provide.

For insurance to be obtained, a proposed or existing structure must be certified in relation to the base flood elevation. A licensed land surveyor must provide a floodway certification survey to determine the BFE in relation to the building site and provide pertinent data back to the local agency for approval.

Your local county or city public works department keeps copies of FIRM maps. They can also be viewed and copies purchased if necessary at: FEMA's Web site (msc.fema.gov).

If either purchasing a new parcel or researching one you already own, it is wise to have a licensed land surveyor check into the possibility of being within the floodway.

While the dangers of flooding are more predictable with the current FIRM mapping, it never hurts to do some additional checking with local owners. Finding the original owner that's lived in the area for decades can be a wealth of information in how an area has flooded in the past.

Moving Forward

Up to this point, we've taken a look at some of the various ways property rights and value can be lost, and how to identify potential problems Now, let's take a look at how to research the condition of an existing or prospective piece of property.

CHAPTER 8 – KEY POINTS

✓ An Act of God is considered an overwhelming, unpreventable event caused exclusively by forces of nature, such as in earthquake, flood, or tornado. The definition has been statutorily broadened to include all natural phenomena that are exceptional, inevitable, and irresistible, the effects of which could not be prevented or avoided by the exercise of due care or foresight.

✓ Insurance transfers the liability of a loss from one party to another in exchange for a premium. To be successful, insurers have to be experts at calculating levels of risk, charging enough to make a profit from premiums while still compensating for damages. On the insurers' side of the fence, this is considered the law of large numbers, which is purely based on the laws of probability and statistics, showing that as the number of exposed units increases, the likelihood of predicting an expected result increases also.

✓ Flood and earthquake insurance are typically not covered in a standard homeowner's insurance policy. These are separate policies a buyer should purchase in certain areas.

✓ To mitigate flood damage to existing homes, as well as provide protection for new ones, the federal government stepped in, implementing the Flood Disaster Protection Act in 1973. This act is administrated by the Flood Emergency Management Agency, better known as FEMA.

✓ Land surveyors determine whether existing buildings or future building sites are within the floodway. Sometimes it may not be discovered that a structure is in or near the floodway until an owner tries to sell or refinance their home. Bank regulatory agencies and secondary market agencies (e.g. Fannie Mae and Freddie Mac) are responsible for enforcing the law by requiring borrowers to obtain flood insurance for the extent of their loans.

9

Records Research

If we knew what it was we were doing, it would not be called research would it? Albert Einstein

To research the history of a parcel of land, one must realize there are various departments with different functions within a typical county government. Here's a list of each common major department and a brief breakdown on the function they perform:

1. **The Assessor's Office** – You guessed it: This office determines how much your land is worth and, depending on where you live, it may be in charge of collecting property taxes.

2. **The Drafting Office** – This office drafts the maps that show all the parcels within a county. These maps are usually assessment maps and are a tool for each department to track the size, position, and zoning of

a parcel

3. **The Recorder's Office** – This is the where documents are officially recorded. Deeds, easements, marriage records, birth and death certificates, etc., are filed here to give what is called constructive notice of an action. This office typically holds copies of these documents, as well as tracking books and software to allow for organization as well as research. The county's grantor and grantee indexes are housed here as well.

4. **The Planning Office** – This office deals primarily with approving land improvement or development. County land planners guide landowners through the proper process to change or develop their land. Within this office are separate divisions, such as the Building Department, who approves structures and issues construction permits.

5. **The Public Works or Roads Office** – This office develops and maintains the county's roads, bridges, and utilities. Usually this office is broken down into sub-departments, such as engineering and maintenance. They design, construct, and maintain the county's infrastructure. Sometimes, this department will merely manage private companies that they've hired to perform these tasks. The maintenance division may be located at a separate location due to its need for space for snowplows, road graders, and the like. One will often find maps showing county

road rights-of-way in this office.

6. **The Surveyor's Office** – The County Surveyor reviews and approves all surveys performed within a county. Sometimes, larger cities will review and approve surveys within their jurisdiction, but all approved surveys are still filed with the County Surveyor's office. Once recorded, surveys are sent to Drafting and Recorder's offices to update their mapping.

7. **Geographic Information Systems or GIS** – Counties with a large enough tax base typically now have departments that construct computer databases to bring the records of all the departments together into one single interface. A GIS typically is constructed with software that links a records database with an interactive map. County staff and the public can access the GIS, zoom the map to a parcel, select it, and find out everything about that parcel. One can even turn on aerial photos and overlay other maps such as floodways, city limit lines, rights-of-way, etc. As with assessment mapping, however, the lines shown in a GIS are only approximate, and may be off by many feet.

As you can see, a county government is a multi-faceted organism that keeps records as well as maintains and regulates the activities and infrastructure in a large area. The county staff works to implement the rules that you, a U.S. citizen, has voted into law. These are your public servants, your tax dollars at work.

A first thing to realize is that records research doesn't have to be difficult. One just needs to learn how to get around within the different departments and utilize the resources there. And after performing research within a certain county, one will begin to understand that every county is a little different. Over the last couple hundred years, many changes have transpired in how a county indexes its records; finding that 30-year veteran within a department can be a valuable resource in pointing you in the right direction.

To begin to research a parcel of land, one first needs to determine if your county has an online GIS. If they do, this can save numerous hours. For an example, check out the GIS in my home county, Jackson County in Oregon: www.smartmap.org.

Many counties don't yet have a system like this in place, and even if yours does, it will often just be a place to start. To begin, whether researching an online GIS or hard copy records, the first thing to determine is your property's tax lot or tax ID. number. This is the property's unique description. As we learned in the section on boundaries and legal descriptions, parcels of land in the United States are either part of the Public Land Survey System, PLSS, or were part of some sort of metes and bounds-described land grant from the government to a private party.

A parcel of land that is part of the PLSS will have a tax lot description similar to this:

Tax Lot 100, being located in the Northeast One-Quarter of Section 5, Township 37 South, Range 1 West of the Willamette Meridian in Jackson County Oregon.

Or, a parcel lying within an area defined before the PLSS might look like this:

Tax Lot 100, being located in Donation Land Claim Number 38, in the Northeast One-Quarter of Section 5, Township 37 South, Range 1 West of the Willamette Meridian, in Jackson County, Oregon.

You will notice that the quarter section within the PLSS is still referenced even though the parcel was part of an original land claim. Counties will still use the PLSS system to keep track of an area due to its simplicity, even though the boundary of the parcel wasn't determined using the PLSS as its basis.

Many times, the description will be abbreviated. Quarter sections may be given letter designations, such as "A" being the northeast quarter of the section, "B" being the southeast, and so on. Thus abbreviated versions of the examples may look like this:

TL100, S5A T37S R1W, WM
And the second like this:
TL100, S5A T37S R1W, DLC38 WM

Researching Your Soon-To-Be or Existing Deed

A good place to start is your local county courthouse. If an address is given for the county assessor's office, start there. However, sometimes only the courthouse is listed. Many times the offices containing the records you will be looking for are housed in one local area, and often times located in an office in one of the older and larger cities within a county.

If you're beginning at the assessor's office, have an

owner name and property address in hand. If the parcel you are considering does not have a home constructed on it, it may not be assigned an address yet. An owner name alone will suffice, but you should be aware that the owner may own many properties. If looking to buy a property without a home, you should request an assessor's map or tax map of the property from the seller's real estate agent.

Some of us are a bit nervous when first visiting a government agency seeking information. It's natural for these types of places to have an "official" feeling about them, and are organized in a manner with which most of us are not familiar.

Information Tip

The staff at public agencies are public servants. Your tax dollars pay their salary and the systems they work for were established by your voting. Use their services confidently to gather information and knowledge.

To quell any fears of knocking on the government's door, you must realize that you are a landowner (or about to be) in the United States of America. The county seat is not where judging officials sit waiting to catch you in some sort of folly. It is actually where public servants, whose paychecks depend on your tax dollars, are waiting to serve you. With this in mind, you should feel quite comfortable utilizing them.

Beware of what I like to refer to as "counter confrontations." It is easy for county staff to become so familiar with the county's system that it is frustrating for them to weather what they feel are ignorant questions. The truth of the matter, of course, is that it is not the landowner's duty to be knowledgeable in every aspect of the county code or regulation, but rather it is the public servant's duty to be helpful and guide the landowner. Now, back to research. With an owner's name and site address, county staff can make a copy of the assessment map that your parcel is a part of. Bring a piece of paper and pencil to jot down the tax lot number and description, and bring some cash in case the county charges for copies.

See below for an example of an assessor's map:

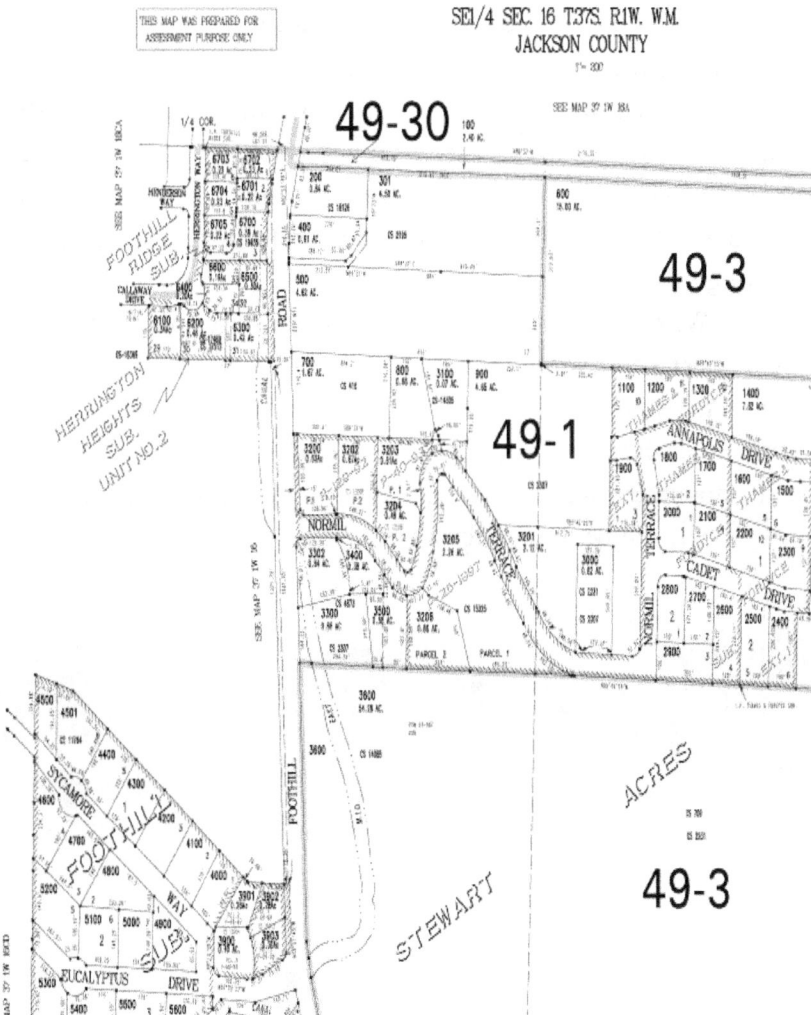

In rare instances, you may find that a site address has a name other than the owner associated with it. This could be because the owner has leased the property to someone else who is responsible for paying taxes on the land.

You will quickly determine that it takes some common sense when doing records research. You have to ask yourself, "what would cause a different name than what you believe is the owner to pop up when researching a property?" Another possibility would be the name of certain family trust, in which the seller is merely listed as a trustee within a deed. But let's be clear: What we are after is a tax lot number and property description, which is the way a county tracks a singular parcel of land. Once we have this, we can move on to the place where the county tracks everything recorded that affects a parcel: the drafting office.

With a tax lot number and property description in hand, we request a copy of the deed card for the tax lot of interest. The deed card shows the documents recorded that affect a parcel. Sometimes they are complete, and sometimes they aren't, but this is the document we will use to begin our research in earnest.

See the next page for an example of a typical deed card:

37/6. /6 /D 5900
16-37-1N-35-2

RECORD OF DESCRIP RF 1 4e445-1

OFFICE OF COUNTY ASSESSOR, .

371w1ED 0S9cc e4909

CODE NUMBER 19-1

ACCOUNT NUMBER

AERIAL PHOTO

	SECTION	TOWNSHIP 8	RANGE W.M.	MAP NO. 16-37-1W
35-2	LOT	BLOCK		
TAX LOT NUMBER	NO.	NO.	ADDITION	CITY

INDENT EACH NEW COURSE TO THIS LINE	LEGAL DESCRIPTION A.	DEED RECORD			ACRES REMAINING
		YEAR	VOLUME	PAGE	

LEGAL DESCRIPTION	YEAR	VOLUME	PAGE	ACRES REMAINING
Carter, Gerry Commencing at the Southwest corner of Lot 16, of Stewart Acres in JCO; thence North 0° 01' 00" East 313.00 feet along the West line of said lot to a 1 inch iron pipe; thence East 120.0 feet to the true point of beginning; thence continue East 90.0 feet; thence South 0° 01' 00" West 313.00 feet to the South line of said lot; thence along said South line North 89° 21' 00" West 90.0 feet to a point which bears South 0° 01' 00" West from the true point of beginning; thence North 0° 01' 00" East 313.0 feet to the point of beginning;	1955	415	6	
Grant, Jay F. & Patricia D.	1956 J.V. 57-	423	204 2249	
Harshman, Edmund P. & Margaret H.	2-5 1957 JV 57-	437 4143	458	
Vessey, Donald E & Beulah A	1963 JV 64-	547 2767	396	
Struk, Daniel Paul & Janet Andrews	O.R.	71-15814 JV 72-	03578	
Burgoyne, Robert C & Dixie R	O.R.	75-14430 JV 76-	01461	
	CODE CHANGE J.V. 83-01104			
Oldenhage, Norman E & Irene L	O.R. J.V.	83-09337 83-04549		

It isn't pretty, but I am afraid that this example is typical. I could have included the rare beautifully and clearly annotated record, but it isn't the norm so it wouldn't be helpful. The information is all there, however, and that is what is important.

From one owner to the next, the chain of ownership or *chain of title* is listed. To the right, the official record, or O.R.

number, is listed. This is the volume and page of deeds that have been recorded that have transferred ownership of the parcel down through the ages.

In the old days, records were simply put down in order by book and page, or volume and page, such as volume 72, page 65 of the County Deed Records. The title for records will differ from one county to the next, but it will likely be something like "County Deed Records," or "Official Records of Such-and-Such County," or "Official Records in the Office of the Such-and-Such in Such-and-Such County."

Even within one county, the title of the records may change over the years. In some instances, records may be categorized in a more chronological nature, entitled an instrument, recorded first by year and then by order of recording, such as a Instrument Number 2008-0001, for the first record of 2008.

Regardless of the local title, the official records find their home in the County Recorder's Office.

The Recorder's Office

As its title suggests, this is the place where the public gives notice to their actions. All the records listed on a deed card are here. Also, all the records listed as encumbrances within your title report (the document prepared by a title company when preparing to aid in transferring ownership) can be found within the cold steel cabinets and computer hard drives of this office.

The historical bread and butter of this records office are the *grantor-grantee* indexes. These thick books are the record of transfers of title and granting of rights from one property owner to another. They are records that allow a researcher to use a title owner name and time of ownership to track the actions taken within a certain epoch.

Researching the indexes is an intuitive process. They are organized by date and owner name. Oftentimes, these records are cross-referenced, labeled *direct* and *indirect* indexes. A direct index may be entitled the "Grantor to Grantee Record," and organized by grantor name, while the indirect may be based on the grantee.

On the deed card shown previously, Gerry Carter is shown as the original owner of the parcel in its current configuration. The deed card matches the deed index, showing Carter purchasing the parcel with a Warranty Deed in Volume 415, Pages 6 and 7. Now, we also have the previous owner's name of the large tract of land that Carter's was sold from, one William Brooks.

> **Information Tip**
>
> The historical bread and butter of the records office are the *grantor-grantee* indexes. These thick books are the record of transfers of title and granting of rights from one property owner to another. They are records that allow a researcher to use a title owner name and time of ownership to track the actions taken within a certain epoch.

With this information, one can continue to use the index to track the property back to its creation through government grant. To research every action that has ever been taken to affect a parcel, the chain of title must be researched to the very beginning of private ownership. I suggest building a handwritten list or computer spreadsheet with purchase date, owner name, and the document number of the deed the current owner used to sell to the next.

Once this list is compiled, make copies of each of the deeds. The older deeds will typically be filed on microfilm and accessed through a microfiche machine. Have staff help you, as each machine is a little different.

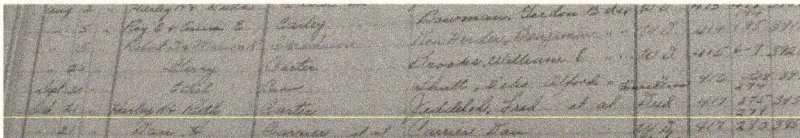

Closely examine each deed. In theory, if an easement is recorded that affects the title, it should be noted on the deed. These may be listed after the legal description of the property, such as a list of documents after a *together with* statement for something that adds a property right to the deed, or an *excepting therefrom, reserving therefrom,* or *subject to* statement for something that takes a property right from the deed.

Sometimes, the easement description itself will be made part of a deed, such as a subject to statement, followed by the complete legal description of the easement.

But typically, just the recording number of the deed that gave constructive notice to the easement is given, such as in the example below:

392040

964372

WARRANTY DEED

Vol.415 Page 6

KNOW ALL MEN BY THESE PRESENTS that we, WILLIAM E. BROOKS and SAM ETHEL BROOKS, husband and wife, Grantors, in consideration of Ten Dollars ($10.00) and other good and valuable considerations to us paid by Gerry Carter, Grantee, the receipt of which is hereby acknowledged, do hereby grant, bargain, sell and convey unto said Grantee, her heirs, executors, administrators and assigns, all the following described real property, together with the tenements, hereditaments and appurtenances thereunto belonging or in any wise appertaining, situate in the County of Jackson and State of Oregon, to-wit:

Commencing at the southwest corner of Lot 16 of STEWART ACRES in Jackson County, Oregon, according to the official plat thereof, now of record, thence North 0°01'00" East 343.00 feet along the west line of said Lot, to a 1" iron pipe, thence East 120.0 feet to the true point of beginning, thence continue East 90.0 feet; thence South 0°01'00" West 343.00 feet to the south line of said Lot; thence along said south line, North 89°21'00" West 90.0 feet, to a point which bears South 0°01'00" West from the true point of beginning; thence North 0°01'00" East 343.00 feet to the true point of beginning,

SUBJECT TO:

1. Perpetual easement and right of way granted to the Medford Irrigation District, by instrument recorded in Volume 130 page 162 of the Deed Records of Jackson County, Oregon.

2. Waiver forever of any and all claims for damages to herein described tract, improvements or crops thereon, against the Medford Irrigation District arising from leakage of said District's canal, or like causes, set out in deed from the Medford Irrigation District to G. E. Pierce et ux, recorded in Volume 195 page 226 of the Deed Records of Jackson County, Oregon.

3. Rights of way for irrigation ditches and water lines, now existing or to be constructed in the future, reserved in deed from Medford Irrigation District to G. E. Pierce et ux, recorded in Volume 195 page 226 of the Deed Records of Jackson County, Oregon.

4. Right to lay, use and maintain 1¼ inch main water pipe, and rights in connection therewith, set out in agreement recorded in Volume 364 page 345 of the Deed Records of Jackson County, Oregon.

5. Right to use and maintain existing 3/4" water pipe line across said property, reserved in deed recorded January 10, 1955, in Volume 404 page 290 of the Deed Records of Jackson County, Oregon.

6. Restrictions and covenants set out in deed recorded January 10, 1955, in Volume 404 page 290 of the Deed Records of Jackson County, Oregon.

7. The effect of said property, or any part thereof, lying within the Medford Irrigation District, and subject to all water and irrigation rights, easements for ditches and canals, and all regulations of said District.

8. 1955-56 taxes.

TO HAVE AND TO HOLD the above described and granted premises unto said Grantee, its successors and assigns forever.

And we, Grantors, covenant that we are lawfully seized in fee simple of the above granted premises free from all encumbrances except as set forth above, and that we will, and our heirs, executors and administrators shall, warrant and forever defend the above granted premises, and every part and parcel thereof, against the lawful claims and demands of all persons whomsoever, except as above provided.

IN WITNESS WHEREOF we have hereunto set our hands and seals this 24 day of August, 1955.

William E. Brooks (SEAL)

Sam Ethel Brooks (SEAL)

STATE OF OREGON)
) ss.   Aug. 24 , 1955.
COUNTY OF JACKSON)

Personally appeared the above-named William E. Brooks and Sam Ethel Brooks, husband and wife, and acknowledged the foregoing instrument to be their voluntary act and deed.

Before me:

Florence M. Byrne
Notary Public for Oregon
My Commission expires: January 10, 1958

State of Oregon (ss.
County of Jackson)
I hereby certify that the within instrument of writing was received and filed
at __ o'clock __ M. the 25 day of __ Aug. 195__ in the __ at __
and __ Record of Jackson County Oregon
Beatt P. Hopkins County Clerk By _Ellen Carter_ Deputy

Page 2 - Warranty Deed.

In that instance, directly below the legal description to the property is the line "subject to," followed by a listing of encumbrances.

That was a copy of the deed recorded in 1955. However, take a look at a more current deed (from 2004) for the same property:

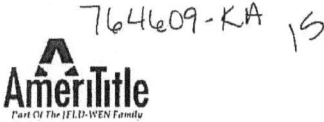

764609-KA 15

AmeriTitle
Part Of The JELD-WEN Family

After recording return to:

Until a change is requested all
tax statements shall be sent to
The following address:

Escrow No

Jackson County Official Records
R-WO
Cnt=1 Stn=1 AVGERICH 08/23/2004 02:30:00 PM
$10 00 $5 00 $11 00   Total:$26.00

010380232004003530500020027

THIS SPACE RESERVED FOR

I Kathleen S Beckett County Clerk for Jackson County, Oregon
certify that the instrument identified herein was recorded in the Clerk
records
Kathleen S Beckett - County Clerk

STATUTORY WARRANTY DEED

, EACH AS TO AN UNDIVIDED 1/2 INTEREST AS
TENANTS IN COMMON, Grantor(s) hereby convey and warrant to **RANDY L. FITCH,** Grantee(s) the following
described real property in the County of **JACKSON** and State of Oregon, free of encumbrances except as specifically set forth
herein:

SEE EXHIBIT A WHICH IS MADE A PART HEREOF BY THIS REFERENCE

The above-described property is free of encumbrances except all those items of record, if any, as of the date of this deed and those
shown below, if any:

The true and actual consideration for this conveyance is The true for this conveyance is pursuant
to an IRC 1031 Tax Deferred Exchange on behalf of the Grantor.
THIS INSTRUMENT WILL NOT ALLOW USE OF THE PROPERTY DESCRIBED IN THIS INSTRUMENT IN VIOLATION
OF APPLICABLE LAND USE LAWS AND REGULATIONS. BEFORE SIGNING OR ACCEPTING THIS INSTRUMENT,
THE PERSON ACQUIRING FEE TITLE TO THE PROPERTY SHOULD CHECK WITH THE APPROPRIATE CITY OR
COUNTY PLANNING DEPARTMENT TO VERIFY APPROVED USES AND TO DETERMINE ANY LIMITS ON
LAWSUITS AGAINST FARMING OR FOREST PRACTICES AS DEFINED IN ORS 30.930

Dated this 21st day of June 2004.

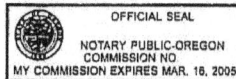

OFFICIAL SEAL
NOTARY PUBLIC-OREGON
COMMISSION NO
MY COMMISSION EXPIRES MAR. 16, 2005

State of Oregon
County of JACKSON

This instrument was acknowledged before me on ____ 6.21, 2004 by

129

EXHIBIT 'A'

Commencing at the Southwest corner of Lot 16 in STEWART ACRES in Jackson County, Oregon, according to the official plat thereof, now of record, thence North 0°01'00" East 343.00 feet along the West line of said Lot to a 1" iron pipe, thence East 120.0 feet to the true point of beginning; thence continue East 90.0 feet; thence South 0°01'00" West 343.00 feet to the South line of said Lot; thence along said South line, North 89°21'00" West 90.0 feet, to a point which bears South 0°01'00" West from the true point of beginning; thence North 0°01'00" East 343.00 feet to the true point of beginning.

(Map No. 371W16D, Tax Lot 5900, Account No. 1-042445-1, Code 49-01)

Curious: None of the encumbrances are listed, which goes to show that one needs to research the chain of title to determine what possible rights have been taken from, or sometimes added to, a property.

Once you've put together a list of all the owners of the parcel of land, one can research each era in which each owner owned the land. Taking a look back at the example deed card, one can see Carter owner this parcel from 1955 to 1956. Researching this time span based on the name Carter in the indexes will identify any easements Carter may have granted, and so on and so forth.

But that could take hours, you say. Well, how much money are you investing in this property? Some of us spend more hours researching our new handheld phones than we do in the purchase of our homes, and by homes I mean the entire package, the land, property rights, and the structure we will build or buy.

Once a comprehensive list of documents is put together, it is time to make a visit to the experts. Each record we discover either takes away or grants a right to the subject property. Once each record is discovered, the next step is to determine what the effect of the record is, where it is, and whom it benefits. If the record grants an additional right, we know whom it benefits, but still may not know where the right sits and what affect it has.

Once one makes copies of each record, determining

whom it benefits is simply a matter of determining the listed grantee. This may be a neighbor, a government agency, or a utility company. Neighbors need easements for driveways, government agencies need road rights-of-way, and utility companies need routes for their lines, both below and above ground. Remember, as a property owner your ownership travels from the center of the Earth, projecting up through your property lines and into space. Even if the power company does not have a power pole on your land, but lines crossing through your airspace, they need an easement.

The quickest way to get to the bottom of the affect of encumbrances on a piece of land is by hiring a licensed land surveyor. Land surveyors not only determine who the easement benefits and what the purpose of the easement is, but they are the only ones who can locate the position of the easement on the ground; there are literally hundreds of specific rules and laws used in tracing land descriptions. This is the smartest route when considering purchasing a parcel of land.

However, it never hurts to put together as much data as you can on your own. Many times, you can determine a recorded encumbrance will or will not be a problem, just by checking with the holder of this property right. For example, let's take a look at the first in the list on our example deed:

1. Perpetual easement and right-of-way granted to the Medford Irrigation District by instrument recorded in Volume 130 Page 162 of the Deed Records of Jackson County, Oregon.

A copy of Volume 130 Page 162 will describe the location of the easement and may give more detail as to what right the Medford Irrigation District was granted in this deed. A trip to the irrigation district is definitely warranted. This quasi-government agency will have mapping of all their facilities. In more rural areas, this may be colored lines traced on large county assessor's maps, while in more populated areas with a large tax base, this will likely be in the form of a computer GIS.

Technology is spreading like wildfire in the agencies. Many government agencies have entire departments dedicated to GIS. Should the agency, in this instance the irrigation district, have a GIS then research will be much more comprehensive. In moments, a technician will be able to pull up a map of the property with irrigation lines overlaid.

In an advanced system, the recording number of the easement may be associated with the line shown on the property. This will help you to determine if the line shown is the one called out in the easement in question, in this instance, an easement described in Volume 130 Page 162 of the Deed Records of Jackson County. This is especially important in a case such as this, whereupon an inspection of the sample deed shown prior, it is clear that more than one easement exists in benefit of the irrigation district.

Using the list you've compiled, you can visit utility companies, government agencies, and even adjoining owners to gather information. This may sound like a lot of work, but imagine discovering after signing that you can't add on to

---

Information Tip

Using a list of encumbrances you should visit the pertinent utility companies, government agencies, and even adjoining owners to gather information.

---

your house, or that the county is able to widen the road out front to within 10 feet of your front door, or that the possibility that you thought you had to divide your land doesn't exist because of an unknown easement.

Many counties and cities have a growing amount of research materials on their Web sites. Web addresses have been set aside for local governments. For counties, the typical address is www.co.(county name).(state postal code).us, such as www.co.jackson.or.us for Jackson County, Oregon's Web site. For cities, the typical address is www.ci (city name).(state postal code).us, such as www.ci.medford.or.us for the City of Medford, Oregon's Web site.

Visiting the owners of easements will shed light on who owns rights to the property and for what purpose. And you will likely be able to scratch a few encumbrances off the list after you determine the purpose of each easement.

To wrap up our discussion of research, there is another key element required prior to purchase: a thorough physical inspection of the property.

If you are approaching making an offer on a property, you will likely have already made a cursory visit. As a savvy property rights expert, you will conduct that initial inspection a bit differently than the average homebuyer. Now, with knowledge of the acts that have transpired to change the state of this property over the past centuries, you must visit the property again.

Property Inspection – What to Look For

While compiling a listing of historical records may sound intimidating, practice makes perfect. And familiarizing yourself with your local agencies will help you in the future if ever decide to improve your property. Consider obtaining a home site approval on a bare piece of land. I've seen this process take anywhere from six months to two years, depending on the owner or agents understanding of the process. A powerful defense against future delays is knowledge of the physical state of the property. It's time to spade the soil and see if any bones arise. To pull this off in a way to gain the most bang for your buck, you really need to change your hat, unless you were born a naturally pessimistic property investigator; in that case, just be yourself.

When investigating a property you will likely have an agent or two on board. Maybe it's just your agent, or in rare occasions, the seller's agent, too. While they make their money selling real estate, it is my experience that agents are professional, informative, and helpful about the pros and cons of a property.

If you've done your homework in selecting an agent, he will likely be knowledgeable in property rights and the pitfalls before you. Agents also have a commodity that some of us lack: time. Real estate markets vary over the decades, but it is typically safe to say an agent has time to do some homework for you, which can be advantageous upon inspecting a property.

Aside from the obvious things to look for, like structural problems with the home, there's a load of possible land mines that can be unearthed with a careful eye. For starters, inspect for the telltales signs of utilities: sanitary and storm sewer manhole lids, smaller lids for workers to clean out sewer and storm lines, and valve boxes for turning on and off pressures lines, like water and gas. Also keep an eye out for metal and plastic boxes or vaults that may indicate power, phone, cable TV, etc. These accessories to utilities are signs of an easement.

You may not think having a power vault near your property corner is a big deal, but where do the power lines go from there? There may well be a spur line traveling under your property line to another property, which will likely mean you won't be able to place any structures near the property line.

Utility companies will locate the underground lines on a property with painted lines. Since the request is not for construction purposes, they may or may not charge a nominal fee for locating their lines. It is wise to make this a condition in the offer to purchase, which places this burden on the seller.

Protection Tip

Utility companies will mark the location of underground lines on a parcel you are considering. This can be made a contingency of sale placing any fees on the seller.

Private lines are not so easily located, and will require the help of a land surveyor to determine the position of the legal description of the easement. In some instances, a physical investigation then needs to determine the exact location of the line, especially if the easement deed gives a legal description but then adds a clause that places the easement around the constructed line. The legal description will give the position of where the original parties thought the line was placed, but ultimately, the actual line controls the easement.

Lines are usually detected by utility companies with pipe locating equipment, which will detect ferrous materials, such as iron or steel pipes, as well as plastic pipes, so long as the installer placed a tracer wire alongside the pipe.

For older, non-ferrous lines without tracer wire, potholing is used, or simply strategically digging holes in search for the line. A more non-evasive way of finding older lines is through *ground penetrating radar*, or GPR. This technology radiates and receives reflections of electromagnetic waves. A computer can then detect differences in the capacity (similar to the idea of the capacity of a battery) of the material it passes through.

The fees for having a GPR survey are similar to having work performed by a land surveyor, and are based on an hourly fee. A GPR survey can run from a few hundred dollars to many thousands of dollars; thus, it is typically only used in unique circumstances. However, if a utility's location can't be determined by the

Technology Tip

Ground Penetrating Radar or GPR is a non-evasive way to locate underground lines. GPR utilizes electromagnetic energy to detect underground anomalies without digging and endangering the utility.

typical, lower cost, and the location will affect the use of the property; this type of survey quickly becomes worth the cost. Again, determining the location of easements should be something provided by the seller, or at least a cost to be shared.

Is there a ditch on the property? There may be an irrigation easement to go with it. Are there overheard power lines? What about a gate in the fencing surrounding the parcel? Could there be an access point for a neighbor to reach his waterline, which runs through your yard? Or could this be access for school kids to get to the bus stop, an access a previous owner granted verbally to the school district? Check for trails or other signs of foot traffic.

Previously, we took a look at adverse possession and prescriptive easements. The physical inspection of the property is the time to check for the possibility of lost property rights such as these. Verifying that the property's deed description matches with the occupation lines (fences, hedges, etc.) around a parcel will require a survey. Some states require a boundary survey for a parcel to be sold, but some do not. A survey may have already been performed in the past, but a land surveyor still needs to locate the survey monuments set previously and mark the lines between the monuments.

Protection Tip

The possibility of adverse possession or a prescriptive easement can often be detected during physical inspection. Require the seller to have the boundary surveyed prior, which will make these possibilities readily evident.

I do not suggest trying to find existing survey monuments by yourself. Many times, there is more than one monument placed in the area of a corner, which may have been set in error, or set by someone other than a land surveyor. Using the wrong monument can be disastrous.

In one instance, when setting the property corners of a new subdivision, a fencing contractor approached me, asking if he could swing a deal with me for some of the iron survey markers in the back of the survey truck. When I asked what he planned to do with them, he claimed his fencing crew often knocked them out when digging fencepost holes, and he would like to be able to reset them.

This is just another way true boundary lines from legal descriptions can vary from occupation lines on the ground, and one must realize a land surveyor does a lot more than just find that iron rod set previously. He analyzes all the evidence and preceding law before marking your property boundaries. Again, request the seller have the lines identified prior to purchase.

A physical inspection after records research will likely

unearth things even the existing owner is unaware of, and it can save thousands of dollars in the long run. Consider determining prior to purchase any constraints on adding on to the home, or building a mother-in-law unit, or putting in a pool, or even adding that shop you've always dreamed of. These can also become bargaining tools during the purchase.

Land has more potential to change the financial status of a family than just about any other thing, so time looking into the chain of historical records and real physical condition of a property behind this huge investment is time well spent.

And for some us, a parcel is more than just an investment in an existing home. We may have future plans to change the existing condition of a property to increase its worth, through such simple methods as a building addition or installation of pool, but some of us want to go a step further and develop our land, splitting it into additional buildable lots, or increase the property's worth through having it annexed into a nearby city, or by changing the property's zoning from residential to commercial.

This will require additional knowledge and subsequent research, which we will explore in the next chapter.

CHAPTER 9 – KEY POINTS

✓ Records research will allow a soon to be or existing owner to determine what rights transfers have occurred for a property. Your local county offices contain the records pertinent to title and rights transfers.

✓ The County Recorder's Office is where title documents are officially recorded. Deeds, easements, marriage records, birth and death certificates, etc., are filed here to give what is called constructive notice of an action. This office typically holds copies of these documents, as well as tracking books and software to allow for organization as well as research. The county's grantor and grantee indexes are housed here as well.

✓ The staff at public agencies are public servants. Your tax dollars pay their salary and the systems they work for were established by your voting. Use their services confidently to gather information and knowledge.

✓ The historical bread and butter of the recorder's office are the grantor grantee indexes. These thick books are the record of transfers of title and granting of rights from one property owner to another. They are records that allow a researcher to use a title owner name and time of ownership to track the actions taken within a certain epoch

✓ Many counties and cities have a growing amount of research materials on their Web sites. Web addresses have been set aside for local governments. For counties, the typical address is www.co(county name).(state postal code).us, such as www.co.jackson.or.us for Jackson County, Oregon's Web site. For cities, the typical address is www.ci(city name).(state postal code).us, such as www.ci.medford.or.us for the City of Medford, Oregon's Web site.

✓ A powerful defense against future delays is knowledge of the physical state of the property. It's time to spade the soil and see if any bones arise. To pull this off in a way to gain the most bang for your buck, you really need to change your hat, unless you were born a naturally pessimistic property investigator; in that case, just be yourself.

SECTION II: INCREASING YOUR PROPERTY'S VALUE

10

Land Development: From Protecting Your Investment to Increasing Its Value

Changing the character of the land you own offers more opportunity than many realize. Land development to most land and home owners simply means dividing their land into additional lots. However, there are abundant opportunities to drive up the value of your investment. Yes, a land division is one way, but sometimes, a consolidation of parcels of land is even better, or, possibly a residential parcel on an arterial street can be rezoned from a residential use to a commercial use, incredibly increasing its value. And, possibly, simple additions can be made to an existing home to increase the value of the land home package.

Even if you plan to live in your home until you die, there are benefits to maximizing your parcel's potential. Raise the appraised value of a property and you make available tens of thousands of dollars to be drawn out of the property through refinancing. Or, if nothing else, the increased value strengthens your overall debt to asset ratio. Having more on the asset side of the balance sheet may give you the ability to get that loan to help your kids through college, or fund that small business you've been dreaming of.

Whether adding a family room over the garage, or manifesting a 1,000 square foot old farmhouse into a 5,000 square foot Italian villa, or subdividing, or changing a residential home into a business place, there are controls that we as a people have imposed on development. For 90% or so of the population, these controls are implemented through local government land use zoning. The other 10% live in areas without zoning controls, living under nuisance law, which we will look at below.

First and foremost, one must realize that within the current zoning standards the community's speculations/plans for the future materialize. Through city council and planning commission meetings, a community gets to shape its future. Its ideas control the zoning choices a community makes for the future, and control where a community's usage controls exist today.

All of the whys and hows of development within a community come from its zoning regulations. And there is a pattern to how these regulations come together. Understanding these patterns, and especially the ins and outs of the patterns within a local community, will allow you to make your decision far ahead of the curve of the typical buyer.

And, as with most rules in life, understanding how and why they came about, rather than just reacting and attempting to comply with a list of regulations, will allow us to prosper within the system most effectively.

Zoning Regulations in The U.S.

Zoning came about in the U.S. in the early Twentieth Century as a means to step beyond typical nuisance law, which was the guiding control system at the time. Nuisance law does not allow one neighbor to interfere with another's enjoyment of their property. Zoning ordinances, however, allow for planning and the implementation of controls over the real estate development of our ever- growing population.

New York City adopted the first zoning ordinance in 1916 to stem the infiltration of heavy industrial uses into existing residential districts. While New York's first attempt at a zoning code was a mere 20 pages, its current code is over 900 pages long, controlling everything from the height of Donald Trump's towers to making sure you pick up after your dog.

> **Information Tip**
>
> Above and beyond our local zoning codes, federal and statute regulations have been enacted to protect our health, the environment, and preserve our historical artifacts.

Most of us enjoy the fact that our subdivisions or rural residences are quiet and peaceful, clean and free from tallow plants and toxic waste dumps. We appreciate that a high-rise apartment building can't be built next to our half-acre Victorian estate.

Without zoning regulations this wouldn't be the case.

Above and beyond our local zoning codes, federal and statute regulations have been enacted to protect our health, the environment, and preserve our historical artifacts. The Resource Conservation and Recovery Act, the Solid Waste Disposal Act of

1976, the Endangered Species Act, and the National Historical Preservation Act of 1966 are but a few of the regulations we have brought into place to ensure the health and history of our species and planet.

Typically, your zoning is created and regulated by the jurisdiction you live in, be it a town, city, village, or county. For a population to develop an infrastructure conducive to the lifestyle most wish to enjoy requires planning. Imagine having to replace the waterline in the street in front of your house with a larger one every time a new house goes up at the end of the road. To prevent poorly designed public works projects, as well as ensure the state of our neighborhoods, commercial and industrial areas are planned well; a master plan of zoning districts is necessary. This master plan is the heart and soul of a community's future growth, and if in the market, a tool in determining where to buy.

A master plan identifies where a community determines is its most intelligent path to growth. This includes perimeter growth parameters, and also may include improvements to existing zoning districts that aren't performing well, such as residential districts along well-traveled routes which are now more suited for commercial/professional developments.

Changes in existing zoning may suit a master plan for a neighborhood, but can be difficult for local residences. Consider a change from residential to commercial. For the landlord that owns a rental along what's now a busy street, it may grow the value of his investment when a house now becomes a potential business, while to the retired couple living on limited income and wishing nothing more than to live their lives in a peaceful residential environment, this change can be devastating.

A broad-range planning map of a community is displayed below:

LAND USE CLASSIFICATIONS

- Urban High Density Residential (UH)
- Urban Medium Density Residential (UM)
- Urban Residential (UR)
- Limited Service Area Overlay (LS)

- Commercial (CM)
- Service Commercial (SC)
- General Industrial (GI)
- Heavy Industrial (HI)

- Airport (A)
- City Center (CC)
- Parks and Schools (PS)
- Greenways

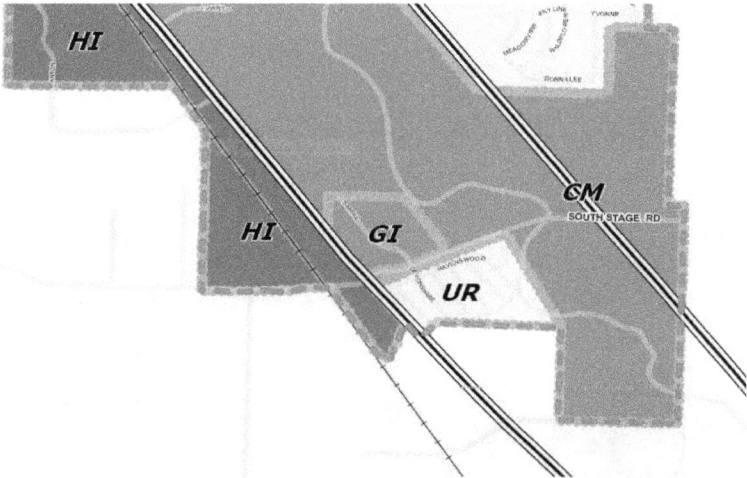

Defined in more detail, see the Zoning Jurisdiction Map below:

CITY ZONES
Residential

- ● Multi-Family - 30 Units/Acre (MFR-30)
- ● Multi Family - 20 Units/Acre (MFR-20)
- ● Multi-Family - 15 Units/Acre (MFR-15)
- ● Single Family - 10 Units/Acre (SFR-10)

- ○ Single Family - 6 Units/Acre (SFR-6)
- ○ Single Family - 4 Units/Acre (SFR-4)
- ○ Single Family - 2 Units/Acre (SFR-2)
- ○ Single Family - 1 Unit/Lot (SFR-00)

Commercial

- ● Heavy (C-H)
- ● Regional (C-R)
- ● Community (C-C)
- ● Neighborhood (C-N)
- ○ Service/Professional (C-S/P)

Industrial

- ● Heavy (I-H)
- ● General (I-G)
- ○ Light (I-L)

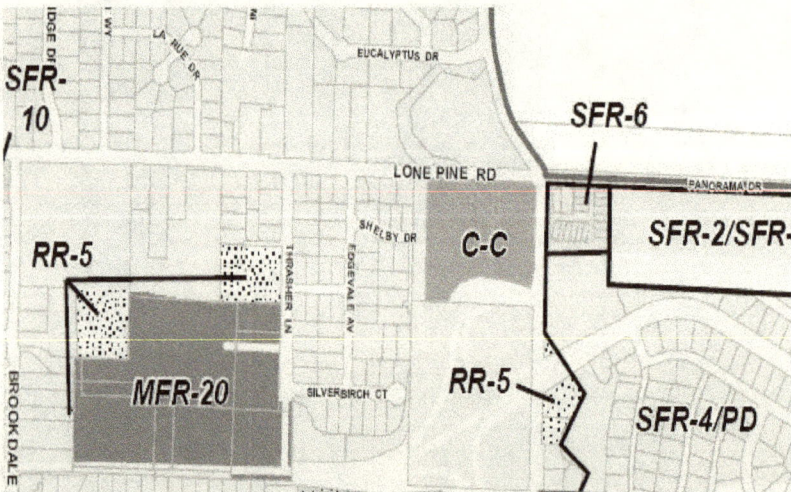

As you can see, the master plan defines general guidelines, while the zoning map defines actual usage boundaries. PD stands for planned development, an overlying district in this specific area.

Complicated? Not really, just the manifestation of years of local planning, which one can familiarize themselves with over a few hours of studying the local mapping. Understanding these districts, and more importantly, understanding the ideas behind the community's land planning decisions, will allow a buyer to choose wisely, and a current landowner to determine existing uses and the future uses in his or her area.

As a real estate buyer or existing owner wanting to determine the possible uses of a parcel, you need to understand how zoning districts are tracked in the offices of local government. Zoning districts, as we've seen, are set aside for certain uses. These districts have many different titles, such as SFR for "single-family residential," MFR for "multi-family residential," I for "industrial," C or CM for "commercial," A for "agricultural," or sometimes EFU for "exclusive farm use," and so on. These designations can be further broken down, in the case of LI for "light industrial" or HI for "heavy industrial" could mean the difference between a district set aside for mini-storages and auto mechanics in the case of LI, or shipping yards and textile mills in the case of HI.

Communities even further identify their residential zoning districts with numerical values defining area allowances, such as SFR6 to convey single-family residences only, and at six lots per acre. And some other communities may entitle a zoning district SFR6 also, meaning in this case single-family residence 6,000 square foot minimum lot size. Being there is 43,560 square feet in one acre, determining what a local community means by their coding is important. After all, SFR6 in the first type of designation would mean a minimum lot size of 7,260 square feet. One will need to familiarize themselves with the abbreviated titles of zoning designation of their local community.

There are two separate schools of thought when it comes to zoning: *cumulative* and *exclusive*.

Cumulative Zoning

Cumulative zoning allows for residential uses within the other districts of zoning, but only residential uses in residential districts. Residential, as the "highest" form of zoning, is protected within its own districts, but can intermingle within the others. This is sometimes referred to as *Euclidian Zoning*, named after a famous zoning case in the 1920s in Euclid, Ohio, in which a real estate company sued the Village of Euclid over not allowing a zone change of a 60-acre tract from residential to industrial. The real estate company, Ambler Realty, won their case in federal district court, the court deciding Euclid's zoning an improper use of police power. Euclid's attorney appealed, and later, Euclid's zoning decision was approved by the United States Supreme Court.

Exclusive Zoning

The second common type of zoning is exclusive zoning, which allows only certain uses within districts, i.e. commercial only in a commercial district, with no infiltration of residential.

Now, let's take a look at the regulations imposed on property usage through zoning.

Zoning Controls

In urban and rural residential districts, the latter of which is the focus of this book, zoning often controls the minimum area, setbacks, coverage and building height requirements of a parcel of land.

Area Controls

The *area control* often determines the minimum acreage of a parcel when dividing a larger tract. Lot size minimums within urban areas often range from as large as one quarter of an acre to as small as one tenth of an acre, which hardly allows for a landscape buffer between homes. Rural parcel size minimums may range from as large as 160 acres in a wildlife sensitive area or exclusive farm use area, to one acre in a rural residential neighborhood.

Setback Controls

Setbacks offer a certain amount of privacy and livability in a neighborhood. City lots will often include different building setbacks for each side of a home, such as a large setback along a street frontage, often times 15 to 25 feet. A side-yard next to a street may have a large setback as well, so as not to interfere with a driver's sight distance. Side and rear yard setbacks neighboring other residences may be much smaller, ranging anywhere from nothing in a zero lot line subdivision, to four, five, or 10 feet. Understanding the zoning setbacks in a district will help a buyer or owner determine whether an addition or division is even possible prior to ever applying with the local agency.

Coverage Controls

Coverage controls simply limit the amount of a parcel that can be covered with a building. Your local zoning code determines the ratio of a parcel that must be left open for landscaping and permeable surfaces, which allow rainwater to soak into the ground, rather than running off into the local storm drainage system. (We'll look at the issue of permeability later in a section on engineering.)

Building Height Controls

To preserve the view and amount of sunlight for neighboring parcels, overall building heights are controlled. Second and third stories often will modify setbacks as well. A second story may require an increase in setback, and a third story may add more. The idea is that the taller the building, the further it needs to be set back from a property line so as to not interfere with a neighbor's right to light.

Private Land Use Controls

For suburbanites, there may be additional controls within your neighborhood entitled Covenants, Conditions, and Restrictions, or CC&Rs. Over 50 million people in the U.S. are required to be members of home owner's associations due to owning a condominium, townhouse, or typical detached home in a community designed with regulations.

These are regulations put together by the subdivision's developer to control the neighborhood he has designed. These may include regulated architectural styles, such as only stucco homes with tile roofs, or only homes with 4:1 pitch roofs, or stone fascia present on 40 percent of the front of the home. Sometimes, house square footage is required to be a certain size, or fences need to be of a certain quality.

At completion of a project, developers pass the enforcement of these regulations off to a homeowners' association. This is typically a non-profit corporation, with typical articles of incorporation, by-laws, and the CC&Rs themselves, or listing of regulations to be applied to a community. Like any corporation, there must be a board of directors who enforce the regulations, oftentimes handled with the hiring a property management firm.

Should an owner not abide by the CC&Rs, the association can bring action against the owner through imposing fines as well as taking away rights to the common areas of the community, such as swimming pools and parks. The association can sue the owner and even another owner in the neighborhood can independently sue an owner for breaking CC&Rs.

> **Protection Tip**
>
> A homeowner's association and even another owner in the neighborhood can independently sue an owner for breaking the covenants, conditions and restrictions or CC&Rs.

Some municipalities are developing mixed-use zoning districts that bring the planned community idea to fruition, allowing single-family residences, townhouses, condominiums, professional offices, and certain commercial developments. The idea is to create a small-town livability within a neighborhood where young couples just starting out as well as more established families can live in a place where they can walk to the supermarket, or maybe even their workplace.

Now that we've taken a look at the regulations that control our land, let's take a look at the process of gaining approval for improvements to our real estate investments.

Approval of Land Improvements

The governing authority of land use within a local community often consists of a legislative body, called a *city council* or *county commission*. Their administrative actions may include approving master plans, rezoning areas within communities, and adopting new policies.

Typically, a community will also include another governing body entitled a *planning commission*. The planning commission is appointed by a legislative body according to the guidelines of state statutes. The planning commission, sometimes referred to as the board, may work to develop the master plan and local land use policies. The planning commission or board also administrates a community's zoning code and local ordinances.

Should a buyer or owner wish to develop a parcel of land, these are the entities from which he or she will eventually seek approval. Prior to any approval however, there is a process a landowner goes through with the help of a land planner within the agency's *planning department*.

Land planners are caseworkers and help an owner through processes as simple as gaining approval for a new porch to subdividing a large tract of land. The process begins with a counter visit at your local planning department. You explain your proposal and a land planner advises a course of action. Many times, a pre-application conference will be scheduled, at which the planner meets with you to discuss the potential of your proposal. While this meeting won't guarantee your application's approval, it provides a good opportunity for staff that are knowledgeable in the zoning code to determine if there are any holes in your plan.

The planning department may have requirements in how to organize your proposal prior to their review for the pre-application conference. This will likely include certain forms to be filled out along with the preparation of a site plan.

Preparing a Site Plan

Drawings supplied to government agencies should follow certain common guidelines that apply to all engineering and architectural drawings. Depending on the complexity of a proposal, many times land surveyors, land use planners, or architects are called in at this stage of the game. However, site plans can be prepared by the drafting-savvy landowner.

A site plan is a plan view drawing, a snapshot of the basic line work of a property and the proposed changes as if it were a photograph taken from a helicopter directly above the property.

Site plans range from quite simple:

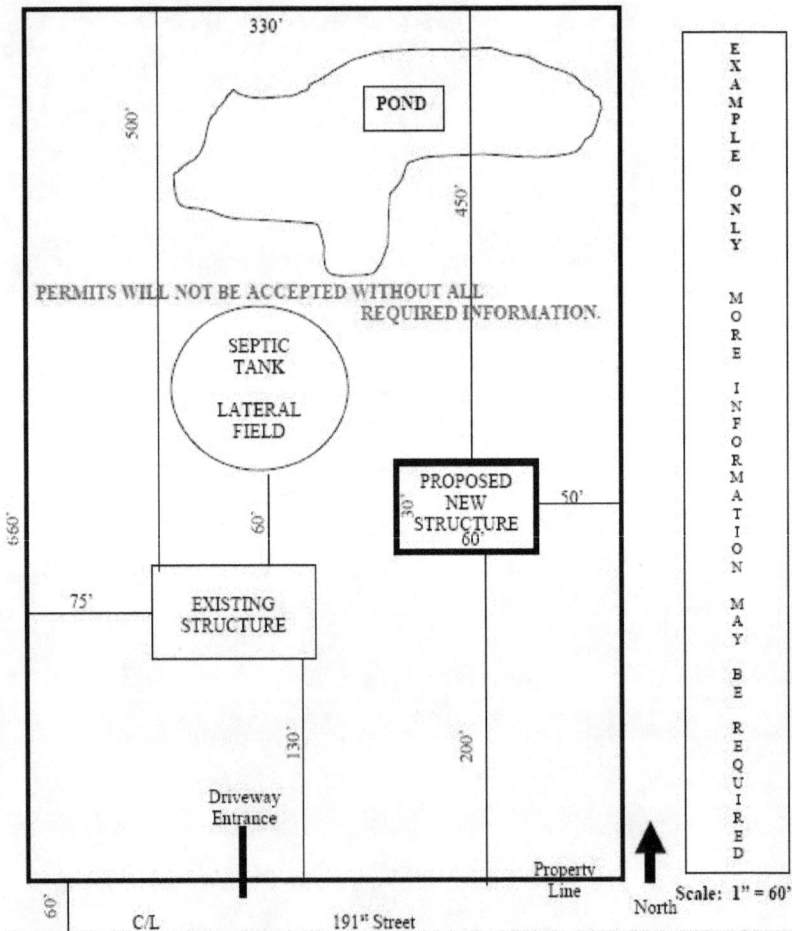

To a bit more complex (this one is from a contractor proposing a new home):

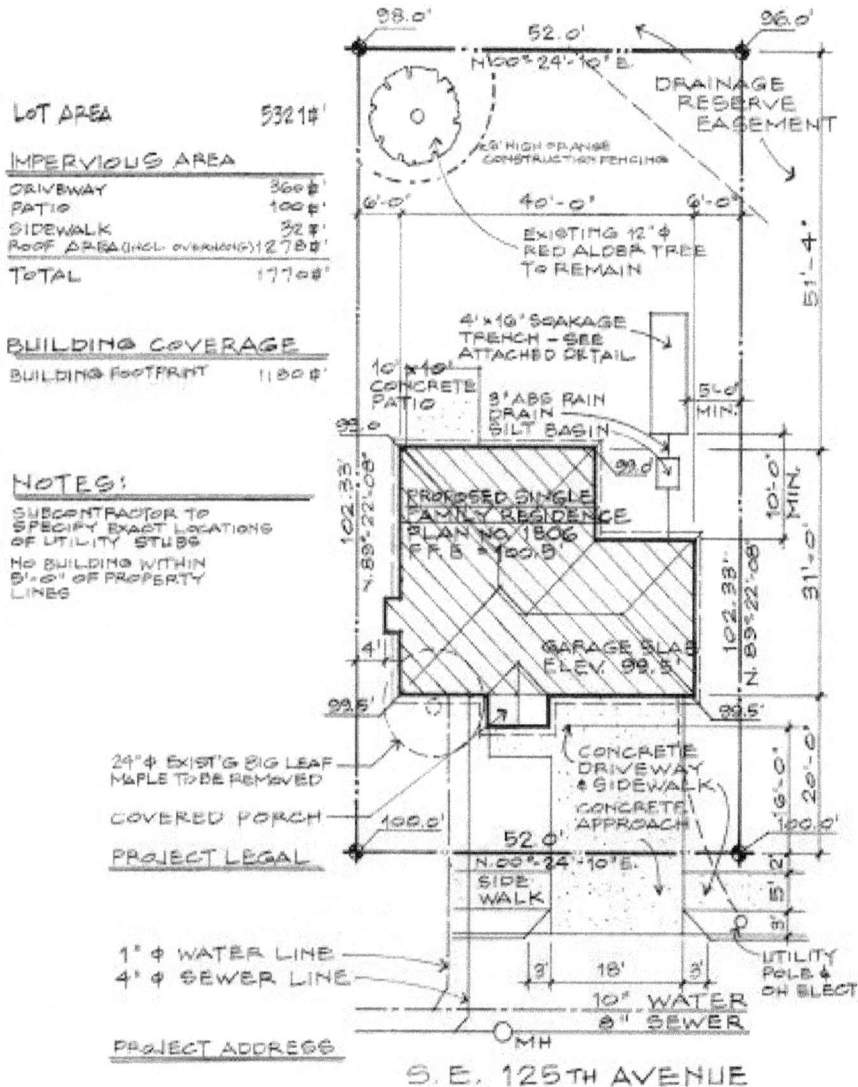

155

The site plan gives a graphical view of your proposal for staff review. Depending on the scale or complexity of your proposal, this and some additional forms may be all that is required. Such is the case with a simple addition of a porch, or even the installation of a sanitary sewer system.

For a more involved project, such as a lot division, only a sketch may be required, at first, to begin speculation. Other mapping will likely follow, such as a topographical survey to determine the site terrain and features, a utility survey, a boundary survey, a preliminary plat map which lays out the proposed lot configuration, and if approved, engineering drawings and a final survey plat of the finalized lot configuration.

As you can see, it takes a team of consultants to take a land division through the ropes. It may pay to visit a good land surveying firm prior to visiting the city or county planning department. For likely no fee they will be willing to discuss the feasibility of your ideas. Next, we'll look more in-depth at the process of land division.

CHAPTER 10 – KEY POINTS

✓ Zoning ordinances allow for planning and the implementation of controls over the real estate development of our ever growing population.

✓ A master plan identifies where a community determines is its most intelligent path to growth. This includes perimeter growth parameters, and also may include improvements to existing zoning districts that aren't performing well, such as residential districts along well-traveled routes which are now more suited for commercial/professional developments.

✓ There are two major types of zoning used in the U.S., Cumulative and Exclusive:

  o Cumulative zoning allows for residential uses within the other districts of zoning, but only residential uses in residential districts.

  o Exclusive zoning allows only certain uses within districts, i.e. commercial only in a commercial district, with no infiltration of residential.

✓ Zoning typically controls the following design parameters:

   o   Area controls

   o   Setback controls

   o   Coverage controls

   o   Building height controls

✓ Covenants, Conditions, and Restrictions or CC&Rs are the typical form of private last use controls in the U.S..

✓ The governing authority of land use within a local community often consists of a legislative body, called a city council or county commission. Their administrative actions may include approving master plans, rezoning areas within communities, and adopting new policies.

✓ Simple land improvements such as additions are approved through an application and site plan submittal process.

11

Land Divisions
John Learns the Ropes of Subdividing

A parcel of land can be divided not only if it has the square footage required for two lots, but also has the area for two lots that fit the design criteria of the current zoning code. Now that we have a better handle on zoning code, let's walk through a simple land division with John, a single, retired school teacher seeking to bring his family a little closer together.

John owns a .71 acre lot within the city of Kismet, Oregon. John's parcel is zoned R4, which in our example means the zoning district allows single- family residences and four lots per acre, or ¼ acre minimum lot size. Knowing his parcel is close to three quarters of an acre, John would like to know if he can split off part of his property and deed it to his daughter and new son-in-law for a new home.

To begin, John visits the city's Web site at www.ci.kismet. or.us. Clutching his copy of *Protect Your Land* for pointers and reference, he looks around on the city's site until he finds the city's current zoning map. John pans and zooms until he locates his property, confirming what he remembered a neighbor telling him a few years back: that his neighborhood lies within the R4 zoning. He then views the city's zoning code, and after some perusal, locates the layout requirements for R4-zoned lots. A fairly simple diagram in the code shows the minimum lot depth, width, setbacks, and coverage.

Next, John realizes he needs a map of his property to start sketching out his ideas. He digs around on the city's site for a while, and then realizes he can't locate a decent map of his lot. Then he suddenly remembers a tip he learned reading *Protect Your Land*, and switches from his local city's Web site, to the site of the county he resides in, at www.co.jackson.or.us. After some searching he finds the county's GIS department. Clicking on the assessor's maps tab, he finds this section of the Web site still under construction.

John hops in the car and travels to the county assessor's office, located in the same building as the county courthouse. For a small fee, the county staff makes a copy of the assessor's map that depicts his lot. While he understands this is not a survey map, it is still basically drawn to scale with his approximate lot layout. He makes some more copies on the way home so he can sketch out a few ideas on dividing his lot.

John's Lot:

On arriving home, he grabs his tape measure and measures his house and the distance over to the fences to be able to plot his house on his lot.

(Refer back to the section on adverse possession to realize these measurements are for rough planning purposes only. A proposal for development should be managed only by a qualified land survey company.)

John sketches his house roughly to scale on a copy of the assessor's map, quickly realizing that as narrow as his lot is, his only hope is to divide part of the back of his property. Questions arise in his mind about how to get access to the back of his lot, and he quickly realizes a division may be possible, but that it's time to get some help.

John visits the county surveyor's office with two questions. 1) Is there a boundary survey of record for his property, and 2) Who would the county surveyor suggest he contact to take a look at the possibility of dividing his lot.

He finds out his property has not been surveyed, but the lot to the east has been. (Check out the map above. In

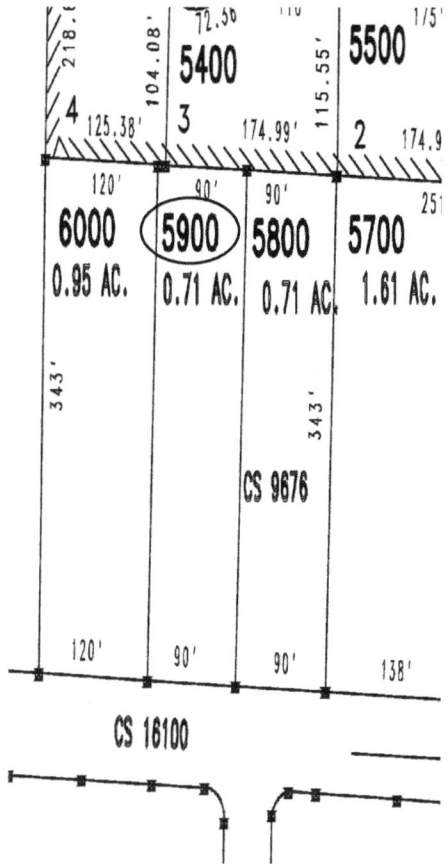

this instance, CS stands for "county survey." Some counties use ROS for "record of survey," or SN for "survey number." Many counties use a different abbreviation, so you will need to check with your local surveyor's office. With the name of a qualified surveying office in hand, you can call and schedule an appointment.)

After a short meeting at the suggested surveying company, the surveyor agrees to throw together a couple of options to look at without charging John a fee. This is common for a cursory review.

Let's begin our look at the land division process.

Feasibility Study

A few days later, John meets again with his surveyor and is happy to learn that not only can the property be divided, but that he can divide two lots off the back rather than one. The surveyor informs John that this particular city allows an owner to count the area between the edge of the road right-of-way and the centerline of the road for the total area calculation, which makes John's parcel, for this purpose, .75 acres. However, the surveyor has learned of one possible problem: Based on John's measurements in the field, his house appears to not allow enough room for a road easement between it and the property line.

The surveyor suggests that enough survey work be performed to determine if the house is too close to the line. If it is, the project may still be possible, but an exception to the zoning side-yard setback will be required. (Exceptions will be discussed in a later chapter.) The surveyor informs John of one final item: He has performed a visual inspection of the property, along with an environmental biologist he works closely with, and does not see any evidence on the ground, nor in brief review of the chain of title that any wetlands or other sensitive habitats exist on the property.

At this point, John faces a very typical situation in a land division: the cost-to-benefit ratio of moving forward with his project.

John learns it will cost approximately $3,000 to determine the boundaries of his lot and the accurate location of his house on his property. John asks why it costs so much when there was already a survey performed next door. His surveyor informs him that the survey was actually for a larger surrounding tract and was coincidently drafted on the lot next door.

The surveyor also informs John that even if they discover the house to be too close to the line that there is a good chance the city would grant an exception to the zoning setback and allow the development. John learns of other options, like dividing off only one lot, as he originally wanted, which didn't require as wide of a driveway easement, or the possibility of what is referred to as a Pad Lot Division, which allows for non-conforming lot designs, but that holds certain restrictions. Considering all the possible options, John decides to move forward with the survey.

Boundary & Topographical Survey

John is disappointed to find out his home is two feet too close to his property line. The good news: The occupation lines, in this case fence lines, fit well with his parcel's described boundary, so he doesn't have to worry about adverse possession. After some consultation with his surveyor, he decides to try for a driveway easement width reduction exception with two standard lots, and then fall back on the non-conforming Pad Lot idea if needed, as he's learned from speaking to a real estate agent friend of his that Pad Lots aren't worth quite as much as standard lots.

The surveyor creates a topographical survey with the site features added. To prepare for their application to the city, the surveyor adds line work showing the planned lot design.

The map is pretty busy. John's neighborhood is pretty old, having once been a farming district, which now is incorporated into the city. He learns he will be required to dedicate a certain amount of land along the street to the city for right-of-way. This is fairly typical along existing streets when performing a land division. Many times, a city will require wider right-of-way widths as a street grows to accommodate more traffic. If there aren't any pressing plans to widen the road, they are happy to attain right-of-way as a requirement of developing your land. You may be entitled to compensation for the right-of-way dedication, which your land surveyor should check into.

Pre-Application Conference

John joins his surveyor at the pre-app conference. A planner from the city looks over his surveyor's work to date, and is in agreement that an exception will likely be granted, due to the city's liking of what they consider infill of the city's infrastructure. In other words, the city likes developments that bring parcels more in conformity with their zoning jurisdiction. The surveyor discusses the way to approach the development, taking his time in getting the planner's feedback on things such as access and utilities. At the close of the meeting, the surveyor makes additional visits to the engineering department to look into the available utilities close by your property and makes one final stop at the fire chief's office to verify the potential driveway design meets code.

At lunch, the surveyor lays out the rest of the division process. To proceed, a preliminary subdivision plat will need to be prepared, along with an application for the division and the exception.

Preliminary Plat, Land Division Application
& Exception Application

The surveyor explains to John that to prepare a preliminary plat and application for submittal to the city will cost an additional $2,000, as well as fees, which in this instance are an additional $600. For the exception, the surveyor will require an additional $400 for filling out the proper forms and the city fees will be $250.

Excited about the project's potential, John signs a contract to move forward.

The preliminary plat map basically provides information for the city's review. The lot design, driveway and utility locations, as well as the new easements are shown. Also, the plat shows any encumbrances on the parcel taken from a preliminary title report as well as the surveyor's research. This allows planning staff to review the development for zoning code compliance. The application gives the description of the proposal and all other pertinent information as to the location, ownership, etc. of the parcel to be developed.

An additional application is made for the exception, which requests a reduction in the driveway easement width from 20 feet to 18 feet to allow for the fact that John's house is only 28 feet from the property line. The city requires an 18 foot-wide paved driveway within a 20 foot-wide easement, so the surveyor decides reducing the driveway easement is the exception to code to request.

Once the package is completed, it is delivered to the city, and if all is found to be in compliance, will be sent to the city planning commission for approval.

A month later, John attends the planning commission meeting. He is surprised to find a lengthy discussion over the exception request. The commission turns down the exception based on the fact that the fire department, while only requiring an 18 foot paved section of driveway, wishes to have the entire 20 foot-wide strip in easement. The required driveway section actually has a one-foot gravel shoulder on each side, which a fire truck can use if necessary.

Chagrined over the denial, and a bit miffed at his surveyor for not foreseeing this, John meets with his surveyor after the hearing. The surveyor claims that there is still hope, for an exception to the side-yard setback distance of 10 feet may still be agreeable to the city. However, a new exception application will need to be prepared and submitted prior to the next planning commission meeting. Realizing he doesn't see a better alternative, John agrees.

One month later, the exception is approved. It's been three months since starting the process, and John quickly realizes that there is still a long way to go.

Engineering

During the preliminary plat process, a land surveyor verifies the location of the closest utilities to the site. The preliminary plat will show sanitary sewer lines, storm sewer lines, water, gas, power, phone, cable TV, or the lack of any. For county developments, on-site sewer disposal and a well may be required. But in this instance, to meet the city's requirements for utility and access design, engineering plans must be developed by a registered civil engineer. He or she will develop plans that define the final site elevations and utility connections.

An example:

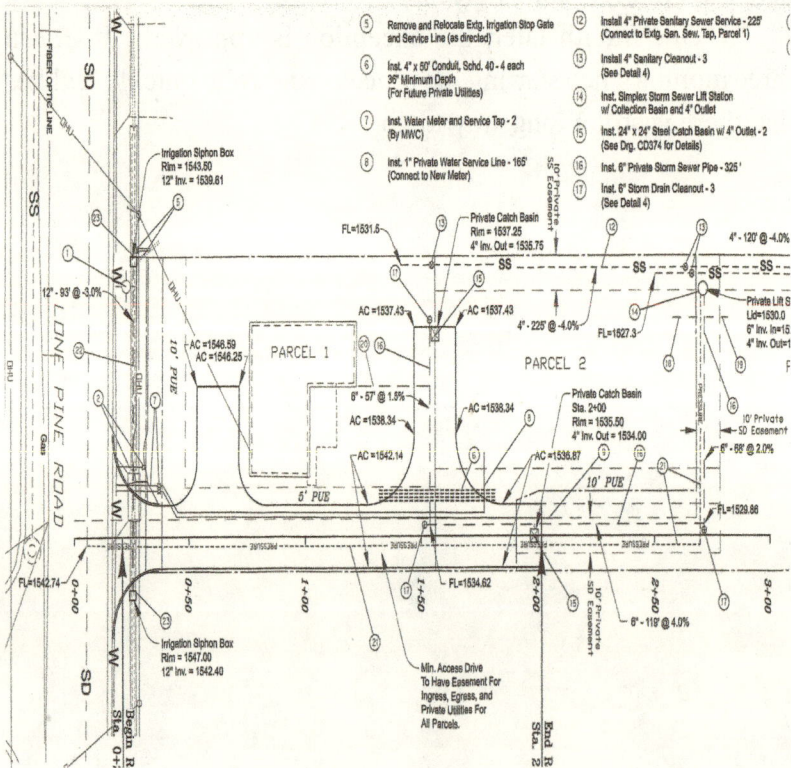

The process of engineering design not only determines the locations of utility connections, but also that the systems in place have the capacity to handle the additional hook-ups.

John visits a civil engineer recommended by his surveyor. Upon meeting with the engineer, John learns that not only will the city require civil engineering plans for the project, but also an analysis of the storm sewer system John needs to tap into for his additional lots. This includes determining the impermeable area that his project will be creating, or areas such as rooftops and paved driveways that would take up space that storm water would otherwise soak into during heavy rains. This is water that will now be introduced into the city's system, and they would like assurance that the system can handle it.

John is curious why the city didn't install a system that could handle full zoning density, but hey, what does he know. He learns engineering for his project will cost approximately $9,000, give or take a few hundred bucks.

Feeling a bit overwhelmed, he takes a few days to think, but in the end, decides to move forward. His engineer develops plans and works with the city and utility companies to gain engineering approval for John's project. Three months later, his plans are signed off by the city, at which point, John meets with his surveyor to determine what to do next.

Project Development

John learns his new lots won't actually be created until all site improvements shown in his engineering drawings are completed and signed off on by the city. He also learns his surveyor will prepare a final plat map of the land division, which must be signed by all the governing authorities, utilities, and any lien holders. At each milestone, John remembers his surveyor mentioning these steps, which now seem to have been uttered years ago in some far away land, where real estate development spelled riches for savvy landowners. Final plat cost: $3,000, more or less. But that is the least of John's worries, for it's time to get a contractor on board to complete the improvements.

Construction

John sends plans to three separate contractors, and as they are busy, it's a few weeks before he hears back from them. The work entails site grading, hooking the new lots to the sanitary sewer, the storm sewer, gas, power grid, phone lines, and cable, as well as building over 100 feet of private roadway. The average of the three estimates: $90,000.

After a quick visit to his doctor to have his heart checked, John returns home. He wasn't unaware of construction costs, but from conversations he'd had with a couple of builders, he'd understood the cost to be about $20,000 to $25,000 per lot. What he didn't realize was that there would need to be improvements made to his existing home, e.g. the sanitary sewer and storm sewer systems on his remaining lot would need to be brought up to standard as well. And, construction costs were currently rising.

To continue with his project John would need to get a construction loan.

The next day, John speaks with his mortgage lender and learns two very important things: 1) The bank that holds his mortgage doesn't give construction loans on bare land, and 2) As the primary lien holder on his property, they would need to approve the land division. Technically, by dividing off the two lots, his bank was losing part of the collateral against his mortgage. They would need to appraise his home minus the two lots to make sure John had enough equity remaining in the smaller lot to secure the debt. If not, John may have to pay down his mortgage to satisfy his bank.

Additional Financing

John calls his surveyor, and after grumbling a bit about not being told about possibly having to pay down his mortgage, asks for advice. His surveyor gives him the name of a mortgage broker that works in land development.

From the mortgage broker, John learns that one possible solution is to refinance his home and to secure the loan with only the portion of his property that will be remaining after the development. John is curious how this would work, as technically, the land would not be divided yet. The broker assures him that this is commonplace. The broker claims it is not against the law to record a deed, a mortgage deed in this case, with the remaining lot of the future development securing the loan. The mortgage broker has an appraisal done on John's property and determines that with John's stellar credit, refinancing, as well as securing funds for construction, is within reach.

Now John is faced with yet another tough decision. With surveying, engineering, and now construction costs, his development budget is now well over $100,000. He has already pushed nearly $20,000 into the project and was a long ways from the finish line.

Not willing to quit, John obtains financing and moves forward.

Construction Continued

John is now faced with the tough decision of choosing a contractor. He's a bit chagrined that while the three quotes are within ten percent of each other, each proposal is different.

Contractor A lists material quantities, labor hours, and markup, which John is able to decipher, but then the contractor details items he is not responsible for, such as permits, systems development charges, and a laundry list of clauses. Among others, the contractor stipulates that if he runs into underground rock, he will charge for any extra time incurred. (The contractor has a similar clause for unforeseen underground utility conflicts.)

Contractor B has a lump sum price without a breakdown of materials and labor hours, but an even lengthier list of clauses that will be considered extra work; and again, permits and systems development charges are not included. While John still doesn't have a clue what "systems development charges" are, he moves on to the third quote.

Contactor C proposes a cost-plus contract, which details what the contractor anticipates in his estimate, but still requires payment for all the hours and expenses incurred, whether he goes over the estimate or not.

John has very little experience with construction, but he once had his house remodeled. He learned enough for a lifetime on that project. No matter what he'd been promised, he knew he was only guaranteed to get what was spelled out exactly in the contract. John smiles as he remembers the promise he made to himself after that experience: If he ever was going to work with a contractor again, he would have a contract drawn up with no options for extra work. He would also make sure everything he needed done was listed in detail in the contract. After some thought, John visits his civil engineer for help. His engineer draws up the contract John desires, and then also advertises his project with the local builder's exchange. John's engineering bill goes up $500, but he's confident the money is well spent.

Protection Tip

A civil engineer can aid in the contract and bidding process to allow additional protection to the owner.

Two weeks later, John has seven bids, not three. With the help of his engineer, he signs a contract with the second lowest bidder. (The lowest bidder broke the rules, placing some creative language for extra work in his proposal.) While many of the bids were higher than his first three, he was still able to secure a contract for $87,000 to an up-and-coming contractor who needed the work. John's engineer proved a valuable team member, checking with staff he knew at the city to ensure the contractor does quality work.

John's next hurdle: the weather. He'd hoped to have the project wrapped up before fall, but it was now approaching the rainy season. His contractor assured him he could complete the work in the weather, but that it may take longer. The contract stated the contractor had six months to complete the work. However, John only has six months left to finish his development, as the city only allows one year after preliminary plat approval to have improvements and the final plat accepted.

Final Plat

Worried about his time constraint, John visits his surveyor again. He explains what they are up against, wanting to make certain the surveyor understands the deadline. His surveyor assures John that he will work concurrently with the contractor to ensure they make the deadline. He explains that as soon as the site grading is done and the major utilities are in place that his team will set the new survey monuments and turn in their work for the city's review. In this way, the city can be reviewing the final plat even as the contractor is wrapping up in the field.

John spends the longest winter of his life listening to heavy equipment tear up his property, appeasing complaining neighbors for the noise, and pacifying the city inspector for mud tracked into the street. He passes more than one night staring up at the ceiling of his bedroom, wondering what the heck he was thinking. He wasn't a land developer; he was a retired teacher.

Over the last few grueling months, he'd worked closely with his surveyor to bring his final plat into concurrence with the city's standards, which included sign off's from utility companies, city, and county officials. But, slowly and painfully, his project draws to a close. The planning commission approves his final plat and he is the proud owner of two new city lots. Finally, he puts a weary pencil to paper and adds up the total cost of his project, at least the dollars and cents part:

John's Project Costs	
Feasibility Study	*NC*
Topographical & Boundary Survey	$ 3,000.00
Application & Preliminary Plat	$ 2,000.00
Application Fee	$ 600.00
Exception x Two	$ 800.00
Application Fee	$ 500.00
Engineering + Contract Aid	$ 9,500.00
Home Refinancing	$ 4,500.00
Construction	$ 87,000.00
Fees and Systems Development Charges	$ 2,500.00
Final Plat	$ 3,000.00
Total	*$ 113,400.00*

Subdivisions from a handful of lots to ones developing dozens or even hundreds of lots run from hundreds of thousands to even millions of dollars, requiring talented, multi-faceted teams to bring into fruition. For our little land division, let's take a look at the following list of actions that take a landowner through the process:

1. **Feasibility Study**
   ✓ Determine proper acreage for division is available. Create sketches to see if additional lots that fit within the agency's zoning parameters are a possibility.
   ✓ Find a qualified land surveyor to perform a feasibility study.
   ✓ If a land division is possible, hire an environmental

consultant to check the parcel for possible environmental or hazardous materials impacts. Wetlands can be mitigated and hazardous materials disposed of, but a developer needs to factor in these additional costs.

2.   **Preliminary Plat Development**

✓ Contract with a land surveying company to prepare documentation for preliminary plat approval. This will include developing a topographical survey with utilities, boundary lines, easements, rights-of-way, etc. The application, as well as applications for any exceptions, are to be developed in this process. The land surveying company will represent the application to the agency's legislative board for approval. In some instances, a more specialized representative will be needed to represent your project, such as a land use planning consultant.

3.   **Engineering**

✓ Contract with a licensed civil engineer to prepare engineering plans for the project. This may include a drainage study and traffic studies if your development will add a significant number of vehicles to the roadway system. It may be wise to get your engineer's aid in bidding and with managing the construction of your project.

4.   **Construction**

✓ Contract with a licensed and bonded contractor to develop your project. Pay close attention to proposals and only accept contracts that detail everything you wish accomplished, being very careful with clauses for extra work. For simple projects, clauses may be eliminated altogether. There are a lot of great contractors out there, but there are some bad apples, too, who seek to make large profits from extra work on your project.

5.   **Final Plat Development**

✓ Work with your contract surveyor as he develops and records your final plat. You can save money by doing the footwork for your surveyor. You can take the plat to government agencies, utility companies, and your lender for final sign offs. Remember, if you have an existing mortgage on the property, the mortgage holder will be required to sign off on the final plat, which may trigger a buy-down on their request. Getting their approval may take weeks or even months, so it pays to involve your lender early in the development process. Other requirements may include giving away any existing irrigation rights on the parcel back to the irrigation district.

Final Notes:

There will be unforeseen fees along the way. When developing capital for your project always build in a contingency percentage to cover these costs, possibly even five to 10 percent of your overall budget.

CHAPTER 11 – KEY POINTS

✓ Zoning regulates lot sizes within certain jurisdictions. If a parcel is of a certain size it may be divided creating additional parcels so long as all lots meet the design criteria of the jurisdiction.

✓ The steps to dividing a parcel include the following:

- o A Feasibility Study
- o An Environmental Impact Review
- o A Boundary and Topographical Survey
- o Meetings with Agency Staff
- o Preliminary Subdivision Plat and Application Submittals
- o Exception Application Submittals (if applicable)
- o Engineering
- o Project Development and Construction
- o Final Inspection of Improvements
- o Sign Offs by Agencies, Lien Holders, and Utilities
- o Final Plat Approval

12

Changing the Allowed Use of a Property

Zoning regulations, as we've learned, control the uses within planned districts in a community. But as we learned in John's land division, zoning regulations aren't hard and fast laws. After all, John was able to gain an exception to the side-yard setback of 10 feet, reducing it to eight feet to allow room for his driveway easement.

Zoning regulations are guidelines implemented by a community to protect its livability and functionality. However, there are many special circumstances that don't fit within generalized regulations. With this in mind, it pays to understand the ins and outs of non-typical uses within a district. There are many ways to change or modify the permitted uses of a property, including exceptions, annexations, zone changes, conditional uses, and sometimes lot mergers.

Let's check out each in a little more detail and the potential they have to increase the value of land.

Exceptions

As John learned, an exception to a zoning ordinance is a small break from the standard. When it came to an exception to the width of the proposed future private drive easement, it was declined due to a possible safety hazard in narrowing the area where a fire truck may need maneuver. But the planning commission passed an exception to narrow slightly a side yard setback.

In this instance, there is no evident harm to the public good by slightly narrowing the side-yard width. And, the good of the public is served through infill of the city infrastructure. (Remember, infill is development that brings larger lots closer to the intended use within a specific zoning district.)

An exception will not be granted to increase the monetary value of a property.

Annexations

The process of annexation is the process of changing the jurisdictional governing agency for a property; for example, a proposal for a property to move from within a county to within a city. The boundaries of counties in the current era are fairly fixed. As we saw early on, sometimes as the country was settling into its jurisdictional areas, state and county boundaries changed more often. Now, county and state boundaries are more or less fixed.

But municipalities continue to grow, their borders expanding to take in more of the countryside as our population increases. Our society has opted not to increase density in our rural areas for the most part, rather the opposite in order to preserve our wildlife habitat. With this in mind, our cities, towns, and villages, our zoning districts designed for efficient density, are growing, and it is along the city limit boundaries that annexations are possible.

The legislative bodies of municipal governments design the best possible growth patterns to guarantee the health, safety, and living quality of their current and future citizens. Within our exponentially growing population, the

> **Information Tip**
>
> Buying just outside the city limits often offers opportunities to purchase land with the potential to grow considerably in value through annexation. A typical two-acre lot along the city limits could have the potential to be twelve or more city lots.

perimeter regions of our cities are the primary or at least most available areas to buy new homes.

Many don't realize that buying just outside the city limits often offers opportunities to purchase land with the potential to grow considerably in value through annexation. A typical two-acre lot along the city limits could have the potential to be twelve or more city lots.

As we've seen, developing can be difficult, but how difficult is it to buy a fixer-upper in these areas as a rental just to sell after the annexation to a land developer? But if it was that great a deal, you ask, why doesn't a land developer just buy this parcel to begin with? Many times they do. Large developers will buy larger tracts with the most potential.

Larger developments are often required to expand city infrastructure to gain approval, which may include improving water and sewer lines for a lengthy route away from the site, such as upgrading an entire storm sewer system or new traffic signals, both of which can cost in the hundreds of thousands of dollars.

Smaller developers will be looking for properties that don't require such a large investment, such as parcels of a few acres in size that are close to city utilities and access.

So where does that leave you? Well, yes, the large tracts may be accounted for, and many of the smaller tracts as well. But there are likely other lots along the city boundaries that may have tens or hundreds of thousands of dollars of growth potential available. However, just because a property lies along a city limit line does not mean it has potential to be annexed in the near future. To determine properties that do have potential, one needs to study their city's growth patterns.

Annexations often happen to accommodate proposals for major developments; they also happen when groups of landowners seeking city services petition to be incorporated. When a city receives a petition for annexation, both the zoning regulatory and legislative boards meet to discuss the proposal. The boards take a look at the existing infrastructure adjoining the properties to determine if the city services can handle the new lots. They also check to verify that the growth patterns are conducive to sound planning principles.

Cities also try to avoid leaving islands of unincorporated land between the city and the new development. And finally, annexations are required to be a part of a public hearing process to allow the landowners in the area to voice their opinions.

To get a better grip on locating properties with annexation potential, let's take a quick look at how cities grow.

Planning for Healthy City Growth

City governments include trained land planners and engineers who work to develop cost-effective growth patterns.

For just a moment, consider just maintaining your own home. If you live in the country, you really appreciate well maintained systems, i.e. your sanitary sewer system, which may include drainage lines, pumps, filters and leach fields, storm water systems, which keep rain and ground water away from your home, a potable water system with pumps, storage, and pressure tanks, as well as power, phone, and TV. Now, multiply this overall dynamic by thousands or even millions and jam it all into a few square miles. In this light, just imagine how important it is to plan our city's growth and infrastructure.

City growth regulations are governed by state law. Cities propose what are typically referred to as urban growth boundaries around their borders, selecting in advance areas that work within the city's potential to deliver water and handle sewage, as well as being safe from flooding and that have minimal environmental impact.

Below we see an example of planning for an expanded urban growth boundary:

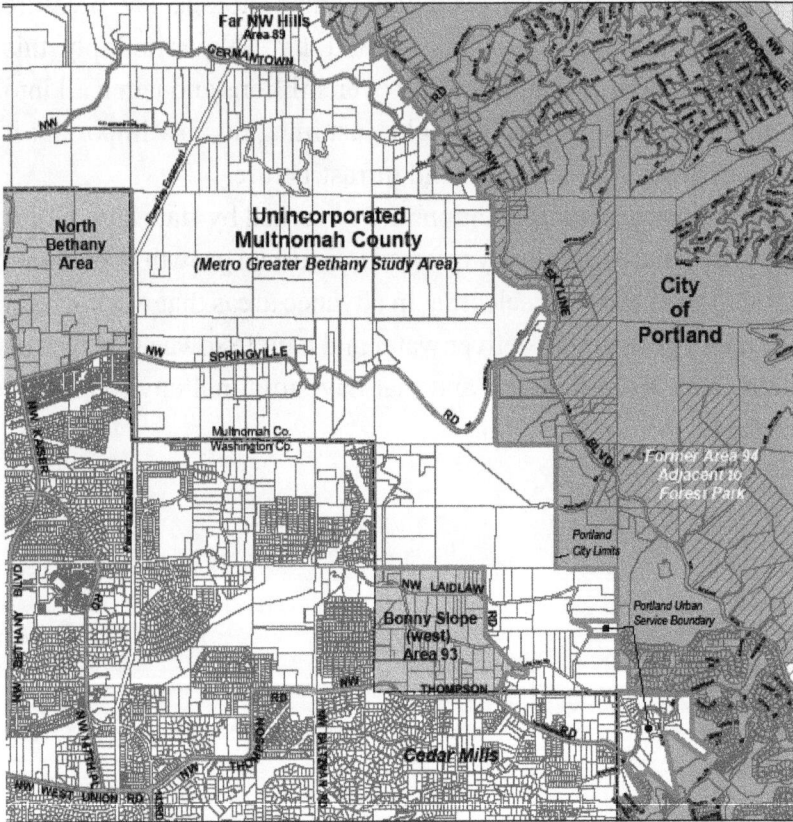

Urban Growth Boundary Expansion Areas Vicinity Map

Legend
- County Boundary
- Urban Growth Boundary
- North Bethany, Bonny Slope (west), Far NW Hills
- Former Area 94
- Incorporated City of Portland

N

April 29, 2008

Planning

1:24,500

All data compiled from source materials at different scales.
For more detail, please refer to the source materials or
City of Portland, Bureau of Planning.

Locating Potential Properties for Annexation

City urban growth boundary maps are generally available for viewing on a city's Web site, but if not, one can view these maps at the planning department of your local city offices.

Another means of discovering areas to be annexed is through attending the meetings of a city's zoning regulatory board or planning commission. These meetings are open to the public, often in the evenings, at certain intervals, such as the second and fourth Tuesdays of the month. Land development representatives will be in attendance pitching their projects to the city. Get a copy of the agenda beforehand to check to see if annexation petitions are on the docket.

Many times, one can determine months or even years in advance of an area's annexation into the city. One has to be careful, however, because annexation does not always mean a rise in a property's value. Check to see what the city's proposed zoning will be for an area first. It might be disappointing to think you are purchasing a future six-lot subdivision only to learn that the city has plans to zone the property industrial, which isn't nearly as lucrative.

Zone Changes

Many landowners and real estate investors have wondered what it would take to rezone a parcel of land. Rezoning, like annexation, can greatly increase the value of a parcel of land, or simply make it fit into an owner's future ideas, such as moving your retail storefront or professional office to your own property, and start to pay yourself rent rather than someone else.

And, like many times when there is someone else that controls or permits what you can do, you need to put yourself in their shoes to determine what will get a nod when you make your request. As it always should be, the agency's primary question in determining whether to grant your request is: Is the change good for the public? The city's zoning jurisdictions in an area may have been in place for decades, and your proposal for rezoning must meet the current public needs and serve the area in a beneficial manner. Will a change from single-family residential to commercial benefit the community by the creation of a coffee shop, which would allow a barista to dine to closer to home, or enable friends to spend more time together over espresso? Or will it create too high a daily traffic count on an underdeveloped street? Certainly there will be neighbors that appreciate a well thought-out proposal, but there certainly will also be ones that are up in arms against the idea. And also, an agency needs to determine if the rezoning is consistent with the master plan. There are many obviously poor rezoning cases that will never gain approval. Deep within a settled residential neighborhood it would be pretty unlikely for an agency to allow rezoning to commercial. But along the outskirts of the community, say, along a busy street that has been widened from two lanes to four to accommodate traffic, well, that could be another story.

Rezoning of large tracts requires a legislative act. An act to rezone a large area will require the planning and development of such an action by the planning commission and an approval by the city council. Large area rezoning may come into play after a major redesign of the zoning code, or because of a proposal for a serious development, like a shopping center or school.

However, for you and me, a rezoning of just one small property of a few acres or smaller is a quasi-judicial act. It is typically handled with what is considered a map amendment. It is most easily accomplished when a property lies on the border between two zoning districts and wants to switch from one to the other. This often will be consistent with the city's master plan. Sometimes, cities develop certain criteria, as in a certain amount of the bordering properties have to zoned similar to allow the change.

A more difficult proposal is what is considered a text amendment, which changes the allowed use within a zoning district. As the change will impact every owner in a zoning district, you can imagine the depth in which the legislative bodies will consider such a proposal.

Never consider rezoning a cake-walk. The best route to success is to visit your city planning department, prior to purchase, if a rezoning is in mind. Without speaking to a city land planner, it would be easy to miss what the city's future plans are for an area. They will also likely be able to disclose to you if there is an established pattern of rezoning in the area you are considering.

Conditional Uses

A conditional use is a permitted use within an existing zoning jurisdiction. This goes beyond the typical home-based business, which allows an owner to use a portion of his or her home for a business, so long as there isn't evidence along the street, there are no additional employees, and it doesn't impact parking. Conditional uses range from day care facilities, to hair salons, to churches.

A conditional use permit will often regulate the use, in other words imposing conditions on the use, such as regulations on hours of business, noise levels, the location and size of signs, and parking controls. A conditional use permit is often specific to a certain type of business. This may spell trouble when it becomes time to sell, for the next owner may have his sights set on an attorney's office when the permitted use is for a day care.

Conditional uses may also require an owner to bring a structure up to certain standards. This may include compliance with the Americans With Disabilities Act (ADA). You may be required to add wheelchair ramps and special parking spaces.

It's a tough sale to think approval of a conditional use will drive up the value of a property due to its specific nature.

Lot Mergers

Owners of contiguous lots within a subdivision may gain additional uses through lot mergers. This process simply joins two lots together. Why do it? Sometimes older lots do not meet current zoning requirements for street frontage, set backs, or coverage. This may allow two vacant lots, thought to be undevelopable, to become one lot more fitting to the local zoning.

Lot mergers are allowed when both parcels are under the same ownership, permission has been granted by lien holders, and no changes to easements or rights-of-way are required.

One can see quickly that any modification to an allowed use of a property comes only after an understanding of the controls in place. Understanding these controls will allow you not only a better chance of gaining a desired use for an existing property, but also help you to select that potential investment property to begin with.

CHAPTER 12 – KEY POINTS

✓ Zoning regulations control the uses within planned districts in a community. However, zoning regulations aren't hard and fast laws. A property's possible uses can be changed or modified through the proper processes. A small change to allow for a land development is called an exception.

✓ Annexations allow properties to move from an area under the control of one government agency to another such as from a county to a city. Under a city's zoning regulations a property may be divided or utilized for a different use.

✓ A property may be rezoned if this change fits with a city's current master plan which may allow a new set of criteria for usage.

✓ A property may be used for a business or a church within a residential district through a conditional use permit. Conditional use permits are often specific to a certain use such as a day care or hair salon.

✓ Owners of contiguous lots within a subdivision may gain additional uses through lot mergers. Lot mergers are allowed when both parcels are under the same ownership and permission has been granted by lien holders, such as the holder of your mortgage, and no changes to easements or rights of way are required.

13

MLS & GIS
The World At Your Fingertips

The Multiple Listing Service is the marketing and research tool of today's real estate market. Many times, local communities will develop listing services for a specific area, such as the San Francisco Bay area of California, or the Portland/Vancouver metropolitan area of the Pacific Northwest. One can search an area for residential city homes or lots, rural homes, or large vacant tracts. One can even further define their search by age of home, size of home, number of beds, baths, and of course, price.

Most times, the MLS is used by an agent to find properties that fit their buyer's needs. However, for a savvy buyer, this can also be a tool to find those properties we discussed in the previous chapters, such as parcels with development and or modified usage potential. This research can be combined with visits to local planning departments to build your own knowledge base of an area and its growth patterns and trends. Just imagine: one can search for parcels over a half acre in size within an area that is predominantly zoned R4 or R6, allowing for a two- or three-lot division.

Once accustomed to the search options and resulting listing data, one can literally weed through thousands of listings in an area in short order, developing a short list of parcels that fit your criteria. This is not to suggest representing yourself when buying real estate, for the benefits of an agent's representation goes far beyond you simply developing your initial short list. However, you are the one that truly knows what you are after, and this allows you to search at your leisure. Once your agent sees the list you've developed, he may have a few unlisted properties that also match what you are looking for.

Once you have a group of properties that meet your criteria, it's time to do some further checking into the likelihood of development, which is done best through using a community's GIS.

GIS

Geographic Information Systems are the definitive planning tool of government agencies today. GIS is not only used by state and local governments, but also an array of private companies, from small land use consulting firms, to large land development companies.

To make the best use of GIS when researching properties, let's take a look at how this wealth of information comes together and how to use it.

The meat of any GIS is the use of maps in combination with attribute data. More than 15,000 years ago, on the walls of caves near Lascaux, France, Cro-Magnon man drew pictures of the animals he hunted, as well as migration lines and tallies, which are the basics of a GIS.

We've come a ways since then. Mankind has

worked through stages of mapping development, learning to mathematically preserve the geometric integrity of land by projecting a round world onto a flat map. Those same map projections, such as the Mercator and Lambert projections, are still used today, although through computer software rather than by hand. Now, we can combine imagery gained from GPS-controlled space vehicles with droves of existing data, all in an interactive, intuitive, point-and-click environment.

GISs are sometimes available online, but sometimes one is required to visit their local city planning department or county recording office for access. Systems sometimes are purely database driven, without interactive maps. With this type of GIS, you will be required to input enough data about a specific parcel to pull up its attribute data. Sometimes, listings on the MLS will not give you enough information to locate a property, such as not listing the site address, which is pertinent to locating a property in a GIS. This is due in part to respect the seller's privacy, and in part to force you to work with an agent to check into a listing.

A property's tax lot and description will also work to locate a property in a GIS, but this information is rarely given in a real estate listing, and is more difficult to use when querying a GIS database.

If the address isn't on the listing, then it is typically easiest to call the representing agent. They will ask you a number of questions about what you are looking for. They also will try to determine if you are already represented by an agent, and if they can show you additional listings. We all have to make a living, and, like I mentioned prior, it is likely wise to work with an agent, but you may not be ready at this point. If you just want the address, then simply be honest. The agent may still be concerned of their client's privacy, which is understandable. Simply explain that you would like to do some due diligence research on the parcel at the city or county offices.

With an address in hand, one can use a text-based GIS to pull up droves of information on the parcel, from zoning to yearly taxes to previous permits.

A GIS with an interactive, attributed map base is a much more comprehensive and intuitive system. The maps include both raster and vector data. Raster data is just an image.

Advanced GIS systems include fantastic aerial imagery from satellite and lower flying aircraft. These images are what is known as coordinate-correct, or in other words, their exact location on the planet is known and their image is placed relative in the map If you are familiar with coordinates systems, you would now know the X, Y, and Z coordinate of any point. Now, imagine that you could take 3D coordinate-correct pictures from the air and then place them in their actual position within the scaled down model. That's what this is. Cool, huh?

Aside from the imagery, a GIS also includes vector data, or points and lines that define the perimeters of zoning jurisdictions. GIS technicians with cartographic and computer skills use computer-aided drafting (CAD) tools to create this line work. Shading is often used to fill these shapes, and then these shaded areas can be turned on and off within the image to see where zoning jurisdictions such as flood zones lay.

However, a GIS is only to be used to get a rough idea if a parcel lies within a zone. If a property looks to sit within a flood zone, it is still not a given that it really does or does not, but rather a warning that if you're thinking of developing the land, you will need to have a licensed professional check further.

Below is an example of a flood zone overlaid onto aerial imagery within a GIS:

In many cases, GIS technicians try to utilize older mapping, possibly derived from scanning old paper maps and then with a computer, electronically shape them to fit inside a GIS. This inaccurate mapping is overlaid onto accurate mapping, and sometimes vice versa. (Early on, flood insurance rate maps, FIRM maps as they are called, were especially grossly inaccurate.) Simply put, a good GIS will give you the ability to check the likelihood of a property's potential for development success.

While there are exhaustive analyses of GIS systems available, the important thing is to understand that the more you understand about property and the recording and research methods used to determine its uses, the more benefit you can enjoy as a landowner.

CHAPTER 13 – KEY POINTS

✓ The Multiple Listing Service is the marketing and research tool of today's real estate market. Many times, local communities will develop listing services for a specific area, such as the San Francisco Bay area of California, or the Portland/Vancouver metropolitan area of the Pacific Northwest.

✓ Geographic Information Systems are the definitive planning tool of government agencies today. GIS is not only used by state and local governments, but also an array of private companies, from small land use consulting firms, to large land development companies.

14

Conclusion
The Importance of Land

There have been few things in my life which
have had a more genial effect on my mind that
the possession of a piece of land.
Harriet Martineau

If nothing else, I sincerely hope this guide has opened your eyes a little to the complex dynamic of land ownership and your ability to gain and lose rights to it.

After all, protecting your land is more than just protecting the trees growing along your property lines. In many instances, selecting that special parcel based on a bit of knowledge of property rights, rights of usage, and our population's future growth patterns will allow for the selection of a much stronger asset in your financial portfolio. This strong asset can be an emergency fund in a tough economy and a resource for your future needs, like paying for your kid's college tuition, or even boosting your retirement fun. Refinancing a sound piece of real estate can even allow funds to simply make payments to avoid foreclosure.

If tomorrow you were told that you were going to have to invest more money than you may make in 5, 10, or even 15 years into a single item, I hope now you might take a bit more time to make the decision than you would buying your next sedan.

In fact, I know you will.

I thank you for taking the time to read this guide, and I wish you well in all your adventures in land ownership. In closing, I will leave you with a quote:

*My own recipe for world peace is a little bit of
land for everyone.*
Gladys Taber

Bibliography

1. Land Title Origins – A tale of Force and Fraud, Alfred N. Chandler
2. Writing Legal Descriptions – Wattles
3. International Internet Genealogical Society University – US Land & Property Research
4. Brown's Boundary Control and Legal Principles – Fifth Edition, Walter G. Robillard, Donald A. Wilson
5. Black's Law Dictionary – Eighth Edition, Brian A. Garner, Editor in Chief
6. Legal Dictionary – thefreedictionary.com
7. www.fema.gov The Federal Emergency Management Association's website
8. Land Use Controls and Property Rights – A Guide for Real Estate Professionals, John P. Lewis
9. Mortgage Confidential, David Reed
10. Neighbor Law – Fences, Trees, Boundaries & Noise, Sixth Edition, Cora Jordan & Emily Doskow
11. 100 Questions Every First-Time Home Buyer Should Ask, Third Edition, Ilyce R. Glink
12. www.smartmap.org, Jackson County Oregon's GIS website
13. Insurance Information Institute www.iii.org
14. National Flood Insurance Program, Program Description, Aug 1st, 2002, FEMA

www.ingramcontent.com/pod-product-compliance
Lightning Source LLC
Chambersburg PA
CBHW020355270326
41926CB00007B/410